The Potts' Factor
Versus
Murphy's Law

By STANLEY POTTS

The Potts' Factor
Versus
Murphy's Law

By Stanley Potts

Copyright 2001 by Stanley V. Potts

ISBN 1-931291-04-7 (softcover)
ISBN 1-931291-09-8 (hardcover)

Library of Congress Catalog Control Number 2001-088442

Published in the United States of America

ALL RIGHTS RESERVED

No part of this publication may be reproduced, stored in a retrieval system, or transmitted in any form or by any means without the prior written permission of the copyright owner or the publisher.

STONEYDALE PRESS PUBLISHING COMPANY
523 Main Street • P.O. Box 188
Stevensville, Montana 59870
Phone: 406-777-2729

Don Gray and Stan Potts just before Don joined the Navy.

Dedication

First, I am dedicating this book to my brother, Don Gray, who died March 8, 1995. (He was born on June 15, 1923.) He was my hero the first half of my life, and I was his hero the last half of his life.

He was a typical restless 17 year old when he went off to join the Navy. He lied about his age and enlisted on January 22, 1941. This was 11 months before Pearl Harbor was bombed. He told me his ship was in Pearl Harbor the day before the bombing.

He had his ship, the USS Lexington, shot out from under him on May 8, 1941 when he was 18 years of age at the Battle of the Coral Sea. My mom and I were driving between the ranch and Leslie, Idaho, with the car radio on when they announced that the "Lady Lex" had been sunk. She pulled into the barrow pit and we both cried.

A few days later mom got the "missing in action" letter. About six months later, she received a phone call from someone who had been rescued and had seen Don alive on the Island called Tonga Taboo (Tongatabu). Our hope was rewarded a few days later with his phone call that he was okay and would be home in a few days for R&R.

He went back in a few weeks and was assigned to the carrier, Shangri La. He was wounded by shrapnel from a bomb explosion on deck. He came home again for a couple of months until the infection from the wounds subsided. Don went back to active duty until the war was over. He stayed in for a while and debated about finishing a Navy career, but decided to become a civilian again. He would have retired at 37! For the next 25 or 30 years the shrapnel pieces still kept working their way out of his legs. Guys like him are the reason guys like me can sit around and write our memoirs!

Secondly, I dedicate this book to the rest of my family – my wife, Joy, who has put up with a guy that probably hasn't been the easiest to live with for nearly 48 years, and my three daughters, Kay, Robyn, and Stani. Many thanks, Robyn and Stani, for typing old dad's manuscript. These girls weren't the best of friends when they were kids, but now I'd hate to start a fight with one of them when the other two were in hearing or seeing range! We have a great family!

Don Gray was serving on the aircraft carrier the U.S.S. Lexington when this World War II photo of the ship was taken on May 8, 1942, in the waters of the Coral Sea in the Pacific after it had been hit by two Japanese torpedoes and two bombs. This photo appeared in the Los Angeles Times and shows the Lexington during the closing phase of the Coral Sea battle. Japanese planes attacked the Lexington, which was standing by for her planes, most of which were attacking the enemy fleet. Several hours later while she was steaming at 20 knots gasoline vapors ruptured lines inside the ship and set her on fire. The fire was fought for five hours, then the ship was abandoned. The picture shows the blast as fire reached the torpedo warhead locker.

About The Book

This book came about because of a bad accident that nearly claimed my life. I guess I decided if it was ever going to come about, I should get on with it.

My several months of recuperation gave me time to do what my family, friends and hunting clients had been urging me to do. They were familiar with a lot of the events captured in this book and, sitting around the campfire or the table, their words at the end of a story were, quite often, "You should write a book."

Well, here it is, and we will see if I should have "wrote a book."

Murphy's Law
(From Webster's Dictionary)

A facetious or satirical proposition stating that if there is a possibility of something going wrong – it will go wrong.

The Potts' Factor

A proposition basically stating that if there is a 50-50 chance of something going right – you can bet your sweet ass it will go wrong nine times out of ten.

Grandma Gray's Famous Sayings
(And a couple of words we have picked up)

"Longer than a Georgia Well Rope"

"Uglier than a mud fence plastered with pollywogs"

"If you get there first you make a blue mark. If I get there first, I'll erase it."

"Taste in your mouth like a last year's birds nest."

"Eyes bigger than your belly."

"One foot in the grave and the other on a banana peel."

"A mate and an odd one." (From the sock drawer)

And my favorite,
"Stink a maggot off a gutwagon"

I "recklemember" them well.

Jess Taylor's favorite saying: "We circumvaliated them."

Daughter Robyn Maxfield
(Upon helping type her dad's book)

"Dad, I almost hated to start typing the next chapter. I didn't realize how close we came to being orphans."

Table of Contents

Dedication 3
Murphy's Law and The Potts' Factor 5
Grandma Gray's Sayings 6
Foreword 9
Introduction 11

Chapter 1
Our Home Destroyed by Fire 13

Chapter 2
First Grade 17

Chapter 3
Early Memories 19

Chapter 4
My First Deer @ Early Horsecapades 23

Chapter 5
National High School Rodeo 1952 27

Chapter 6
The Houston Place 43

Chapter 7
Cattle Hunt at The Atomic Energy Commission 49

Chapter 8
The Angel Creek Ranch 51

Chapter 9
More Experiences While We Lived in Nevada 59

Chapter 10
My Law Enforcement Career 67

Chapter 11
How We Got Started in Outfitting 69

Chapter 12
Airplanes And Unscheduled Landings 91

Chapter 13
My Grand Slam 103

Chapter 14
The *Life* Story 115

Chapter 15
Trapshooting 121
Chapter 16
Bear Stories – Hector 125
Chapter 17
My Big Bighorn 131
Chapter 18
Diary of 29-Day Hunt With 74-Year-Old Roy Bridenbaugh 141
Chapter 19
Sculpting 147
Chapter 20
The Lucky Shirt 151
Chapter 21
Idaho Sheep Hunt 163
Chapter 22
Reflections on Life Insurance 169
Chapter 23
Some Stan Potts Poetry, "Remembrances" 175
Chapter 24
The Long Elk Hunt 177
Chapter 25
The Longest Night 185

Foreword

Stan Potts has been crawling around in the hills of Idaho about as long as there have been hills of Idaho. He looks like, talks like, and smells like the hills of Idaho. He even walks like the hills of Idaho. I doubt he could make it on level ground. And there is one thing more, he loves the hills of Idaho.

That lovin' is something to behold. The hills of Idaho make some mountains look like prairie dog mounds. Stan's love for "the hills" is as big as the hills themselves. This book is about a love affair of a man with "the hills" and with all that he has felt, and seen, and touched, and tasted, and heard, and known about those "hills."

I have admired this man of the outdoors from a distance, just far enough, for many years. He is a man of honesty, but not so honest that he cannot see the humor in the situation or the moment. He is a man of integrity, but not so stiff that he cannot stoop to help a friend. He is a man of wisdom, but not so wise that he would ever miss an adventure. He can find a story behind every rock, every bush, and every door.

I have watched him keep, sometimes for hours, a crowd of back country outfitters and guides howling with laughter while complaining about their aching sides. When he gets them rolling, he has no mercy; he just piles more on. A Potts' session is so fun it is pure agony. They say that Jim Bridger was a storyteller. That he was known on one occasion to keep a group of Indian people fascinated with his stories for over an hour using sign language. In my opinion, Jim would have a hard time holding a candle to Stan Potts. On the other hand, I imagine they would have a bunch to say to one another.

What you are about to read are the stories about the place, collected and written by a man who has been there, and who can tell a story like no one else I know. This is a collection of stories told by a storyteller's storyteller. You are about to have an adventure.

My first experience with Stan was serving on a steering committee for the Idaho Outfitters and Guides Association to serve the educational needs for the industry in Idaho. Mr. Potts was the chairman of that committee. Stan has a lot of fun in a lot of places. But the organization of the Professional Guide Institute was plumb serious business to Stan. The man had the foresight to see the need, to see the corner that back country guiding was going to have to take in order to be of service to the outfitted public in the 21st century.

There was an awful lot of time and energy required in order to make that program work. Stan had the vision. He left the curriculum development to members of the committee that had that expertise. Stan's contribution to that project was selling it to the rank and file membership. It took someone quite "crusty" to talk and convince those other "crusty" folks that this project was important. The result of all that effort is Professional Guide Institute now located on the campus of the University of Montana – Western. The Institute serves the educational and interpretative needs of outfitting in all of the Northern Rockies. And I might add, it does it well. Thank you Stan Potts for that push on the front end.

> Richard L. "Dick" Clark, PhD
> Fellow Back Country Guide,
> Teacher of Wild Stuff, and
> Lover of a Potts Tale
> Western Montana College – Dillon, Montana

Introduction

Some of you may wonder about my choice of the title name for this book. Those will be primarily people that haven't known me very well or very long. If you are able to get through it, you will note that sometimes on my life's trail things haven't always worked in what could be termed "the ideal fashion!"

I will be using a few words that I and others have sort of invented, but that I think you will be able to get the meaning of from the direction of the story. I will also use some sayings that you may or may not have heard, but that I was first exposed to by my maternal grandmother Gray and that are still in use by my family.

I was lucky enough to have had two things instilled in my mind by my father at a very early age. The first is absolute honesty and the second is punctuality. You can probably appreciate both of these values when you get "storied" a bit or sit waiting for an appointment that is an hour or two late.

I have always had an inquisitive mind (sometimes gets me in trouble, no, usually gets me in trouble!) and a desire to build or construct things. I have also had an empty checking account that precluded buying some of the items that my family or I desired or needed. Consequently, you will find several things that I have built which I could have gotten "off the rack." However, most of these items are all of my design and construction, "for better or for worse."

This story contains some of the highlights of my life from my earliest recollections until the present—some funny, some sad—but all the way I "recelmember" them. The "Potts' Factor," notwithstanding, I wouldn't trade this life's memories for anything. I have been blessed with a great wife, a great family, some great friends, some super performing horses and mules, some great dogs, and some outstanding airplanes. Even with the "Potts' Factor" hovering over me, how much luckier can a man be?

I am going to list some of the jobs and trades I have been involved with in the past sixty-six years and counting. These were mostly to "keep the wolf from the door." This gets more important every year where I live, but it is now in a literal sense instead of factitiously! Once you get through the list, you will see that the saying "Jack of all trades and master of none," was expressly coined for me!

I have been (in random order), a pipeline welder, heavy equipment operator, rancher and farmer in two states, and a guide and outfitter in two states with nearly 2,000 big game animals including seventy-one bighorn rams harvested by clients. Also, I was a rodeo cowboy in all events, law enforcement officer, drift miner, pit miner, raise miner, stope miner, winze miner, surface miner, millworker, nipper, trammer, timberman, powderman, logger, and truck driver. Other jobs included, a horse and mule trainer, horse and mule trader, cook, rodeo bullfighter, rodeo judge, rodeo announcer, butcher, auctioneer, pickup man, buckaroo, mustanger, trapper. And finally, a pilot, construction worker, deli cook, real estate broker, sculptor, tree farmer, real estate salesman, land developer, car salesman, and writer.

Some of the things I have done for enjoyment (and some of these made a little money), were and are, airplane pilot for forty-three years. I've owned six different airplanes, three more in a flying club. I am an airplane builder and test pilot. I flew from the tip of Baja to the Arctic Circle one year in our Cessna 180, 2242 Charlie. I hold aircraft single and multi-engine, and commercial and instrument land pilot's licenses.

I am the first Idaho-born hunter to collect a Grand Slam on sheep. I hunted in the Yukon, British Columbia, Alaska, Idaho, Montana, and Nevada. I went to the University of Idaho for one year on a football scholarship, where I was also a rodeo team member.

Stan Potts
Shoup, Idaho

A cottonwood log home with a sod roof, which is nearly identical to the home destroyed by fire.

Chapter 1

Our Home Destroyed By Fire

In the twilight of a spring evening in 1938, a small boy sat on the slope of the root cellar with tears running down his cheeks. He was watching his parents run wildly up a gentle slope, each carrying two buckets of milk. They were silhouetted by the flames reaching skyward from the doors and windows of the family's sod roofed, mud chinked, cottonwood log home.

The father threw the four buckets of milk through the door in a frustrated attempt to extinguish the flames.

That small boy was me, and I was about four years old. This was one of the recollections of my early life – recollections that can still be recalled in my mind's vision some sixty plus years later.

We were left with basically the clothes we wore. My father grabbed my mother's ironing board and my little punching bag stand.

As we lived over one-half mile from the nearest neighbors it was quite awhile before anyone arrived, and then it was mostly just to watch as the weight of the many tons of sod on the roof collapsed and fanned the flames outward like a giant bellows.

As the rumor of our tragedy ran up and down the Big Lost River Valley, neighbors and friends started arriving with necessities that we would need immediately: shelter, food, clothes, bedding, etc. I.T. Perkins, the owner of Perk's Bar in the town of Mackay two miles away, arrived with a canvas tent and wood camp stove. Others brought a bed, mattress and blankets, food, cooking utensils, etc., and we at least were back with a roof over our heads.

My mother told me in later years that the night the house burned down was the first time they had ever taken me with them to milk the cows. She had always put me to bed first. Fate? Luck? Who knows, but this was only one of many instances that it evidently wasn't my turn to go as you will see in ensuing chapters.

Stan Potts at about four years of age, about the time the house burnt down.

My dad found an old board building on a neighboring ranch that he was able to trade labor for and skidded it home on a couple of poles. He used a team of horses as the only wheels of any kind that we owned was a Model A Ford pickup that he used to run his trap lines.

He worked for the government under a program that was called the Biological Survey, probably the forerunner of what is now the U.S. Fish and Wildlife Service. His job was primarily predator control. He trapped coyotes, bobcats, beaver and poisoned ground squirrels with an occasional sheep-killing bear having to be taken care of.

He received a wage in the summer months, and in the fall and winter when fur was prime he skinned and stretched and dried the furs. Every spring he would take the furs to Idaho Falls to the fur auction or sell them to one of the traveling fur buyers. One buyer that I remember very well was Joe Aldana, and he always wanted my dad's furs, as they were fleshed, stretched and dried far better than most of the other trapper's furs.

Between running the trap line, Dad irrigated, cut hay and threshed on my maternal grandfather Herb Gray's ranch. Grandad Gray owned the ranch and the house we lived in that burned down. A short time later the folks were able to purchase a thirty-eight-acre parcel of farm ground for $500 at the county property tax sale. The Depression was in full swing.

My grandfather was a Custer County Commissioner and had other ranches south of Mackay. One of them had a large frame, three-bedroom house with large living room and kitchen.

Grandad hired a housemover named Byrd Tew to move the house about six miles and set it on a foundation with a half basement that they poured by hand, mixing the concrete from sand, gravel, lime and cement.

Grandad Gray had planned on semi-retiring at this house and developing this ranch.

Grandad was a natural engineer. As far as I know, he never had any formal schooling. His dream was to terrace the ranch with dikes and headgates so he could irrigate it in his slippers. He had already started it, leveling and terracing with teams and Fresno Scrapers. What he had finished would irrigate with water about one-inch deep flowing one-fourth of a mile between dikes!

Unfortunately, he had a cancer develop in his lower lip and he died in the winter of 1942.

My folks then were able to buy the ranch from my grandmother, and we moved into the house where my sister and brother and I grew up.

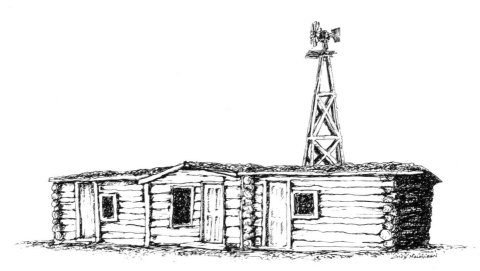

Illustration of a log house done by Chris Malmgren.

Chapter 2

First Grade

When my grandfather started getting sick, we moved to the home ranch at Leslie and lived in the bunkhouse for a couple of years. Dad and Mom were able to help care for the ranch while Grandad was back and forth to Idaho Falls and Salt Lake City for cancer treatments. I think the treatment they used at that time on that type of cancer was to burn it off with radium.

I started the first grade while we were at the home ranch. It was about two miles to where the school bus came by, so I had to ride a horse to meet the bus. There was a shed to put the horse in during the day.

The Second World War was just around the corner. Some of the older ranch kids were going to school and also riding their horses. Keith Evans, a second cousin, sometimes rode with me and helped me with my horse. My half-brother Don Gray, had ran away from home and joined the Navy by lying about his age. He was seventeen when he joined. Keith Evans and several of the other young men left home to go to the service, either prior to or as soon as war was declared on December 8, 1941.

My father had been a miner at the White Knob Mine when he was a young man. I don't remember exactly why, but he was offered a very good job in Grass Valley, California, to mine gold. I think the government was trying to mine all the gold possible to help fund the impending war.

I remember one instance of a situation where I got in trouble for something that I was totally innocent of.

After school, several of the kids would stay and play on the school ground. There was a drinking fountain and several of the kids filled it with sand. I knew this was wrong and decided that I could clean it out. One of the teachers came by and assumed I was the one who had done it. She would not believe me and took me to my folks. Kind of spoiled my faith in the system!

Verl Potts on Champ and Stan Potts on Spyder, horses Stan's brother Don gave to him when he joined the Navy in 1940.

Stan Potts, about one year old.

Chapter 3

Early Memories

My Dad would often take me with him on the trap line, especially if it was a one-day run or it if was so we would stay at someone's house in Pahsimori or Little Lost River valleys.

With the Model A pickup, he was able to get around close to most of the traps, but sometimes he had to walk one-quarter to one-half mile to the canyon mouths for a good set. I was about three.

One time he had parked the pickup and walked quite a ways up the hill to his set. I was asleep in the pickup seat, and I must have stretched and knocked the gearshift into neutral. It was a <u>big</u>, <u>long</u>, <u>gentle</u> slope for a couple miles toward the valley floor and the ranches below Leslie. I barely remember and have no idea if I tried to steer it or if we were just totally depending on luck, but the way Dad told the story was like this:

He has checked his trap and started back down the hill toward the pickup when it started slowly down the slope. Dad was a very fast runner (he could outrun me almost all of my life!) I would imagine he was really hoofing it, trying to catch his only pickup and firstborn son. He said the pickup went a mile or so and run off into a shallow wash and stopped. When he got there a little tear-stained boy was standing in the seat. The pickup wasn't damaged and as near as I can remember I wasn't either.

He probably was so glad everything turned out okay he didn't even paddle my <u>canoe</u>!

My grandfather, Herb Gray, on left; Stella Gray Evans in center, and her husband, Louis Evans. She became a midwife and delivered me along with over 500 other babies in the Big Lost River area.

Hound Dog Fiasco

About the same time and in the same area was another fiasco and the "canoe" got paddled this time.

A big coyote had pulled the trap peg and got away with the trap. It was October – prime fur – probably a $20 coyote, plus a good trap. Dad went to town and got a trapping buddy of his, Orlin Nelson, who had a hound dog, and we went back to try and follow the coyote.

We took Orlin's car, a gray, four-door sedan. Well, the hound dog had no interest at all in following the coyote, so they brought him back and tied him up to the bumper and left me to watch him while they tried to track the coyote out. They were gone a long time, and I guess I felt sorry for the dog laying on that hard ground. I decided to put him in the back seat while I went off exploring.

Well, a couple hours later I went back to the car and the hound had completely stripped the upholstery from the inside of the car. Bad News Little Boy!

Horses

I have always loved horses and evidently got bucked off or fell of my first time when I was about two. Dad had a big, Pinto, saddle horse stallion named Fix and a brown, work horse stallion named Enoch.

Dad had set me on Fix to take a picture and I guess he jumped or moved, and I went to the ground – the first time of many!

I probably spent more time on some kind of horse than off. I was the water boy for the haying and threshing crews, took the milk cows to pasture, herded sheep, etc.

I loved to swim my horses. There was big water several places in the valley, plus the river. I never used a saddle, as you wasted too much time saddling and unsaddling – time you could be riding!

I would ride the horses off into a hole deep enough that it would float them and then either just sit on their backs and rein them where I wanted to go or drop off the side and hang on to the mane until we were coming to shallow water.

I remember Dad telling me that all horses could swim. He was wrong! I found one that swam like a cannon ball!

Most horses could swim with me on their back and the water line would be about on the withers – mid-neck area and their nostrils would be clear of the water by several inches.

This horse was a porpoise! He would sink to the bottom, lunge with his hind feet, shoot out half a body length, blow water like a whale, then

Stan Potts on Fix, July 1936. Under Fix's nose is a grain grinder used to make flour (one horsepower – the horse walked in a circle all day to power it). Photo taken on the Evans ranch. Darlington, Idaho, seven miles east of the home ranch.

sink again. Fun but not smooth!

I also learned that you could fish a lot of the good spots from the back of a horse – places you just couldn't get to otherwise. My dad told me it was against the law, so I did a lot of fishing while I looked over my shoulder. (I don't think it was, though.)

Firewood Fiasco

One time my sister, Marlene, and I were left home alone while the folks took my little brother, Charles, to the doctor for a hernia operation.

We were supposed to get in the wood for the stove, but we ended up playing too long so we had to hurry. She was packing the wood while I was splitting it. I had a brand new pair of boots on, and the axe careened off the block and went down through the boot – through the center of my left big toe and into the sole of the boot.

We ran to the house. I sat down on a chair in the kitchen and took off my boot and dumped the blood out. There were grooves in the linoleum and the blood ran full length of the kitchen.

My sister nearly passed out, but we wrapped the toe up with a rag and were lucky enough to stop the blood. Luck, hell yes! I didn't know anything about compression bandages.

Stan Potts,
about eleven years of age.

Chapter 4

My First Deer & Early Horsecapades

Late one summer, my dad and I were on the range at the head of Willow Creek checking the cattle. There are several bogs just under the divide where the springs comes out of the ground to start Willow Creek.

One of our calves, about two months old, was stuck in the mud. Dad roped him by the head and pulled him out to dry ground. The calf was in pretty bad shape, just lying flat on the ground all covered with mud. Dad got off his horse and went to take the rope off the calf. As he bent down to loosen the rope, the calf lunged and the top of his head hit Dad on the center of his jaw. It broke his jaw on both sides right under his ears.

Naturally, he was unable to talk, but by pointing to his jaws and mumbling "I tink I bwoke my yaw" I was able to understand him. It was about noon and we hadn't had lunch. We had tuna fish sandwiches, and he was able to break off pieces of sandwich and wallow them around with his tongue.

We were about fifteen miles from home, so it was a long, quiet ride to the ranch. We took him to Idaho Falls, and they wired his jaws shut. He basically lived on malts and soup for several months.

As deer season was now on, and Dad was unable to go hunting, he told me to go get a deer for winter's meat. I'd been with him on several hunts and knew how to clean a deer.

I took our brown stud horse and went up Willow Creek with Dad's 30.30. I found three does and made a good shot on one. I cleaned it and dragged it up on a rock.

I got the bright idea that if I could get the deer on the horse behind the saddle, then I could ride home instead of walk.

I led the stud by the rock and was able to slide the deer behind the saddle.

Now, the start of the problems. The only thing I had to tie the deer with was my lariat. I laced it back and forth through the deer's legs, through the D rings, over the deer, etc., until I ran out of rope.

From left are Marlene Potts, Stan Potts, Charles Potts, our mother Sarah, and her mother, Ada Gray, plus our family dog, Skippy. This was about the time of the first deer wreck and the Deadeye wrecks.

I got on and headed towards home. After a short way, the deer was sagging off the right side. I got off to redo my tie job – but the deer slipped more, and the stud decided he'd had enough of this and ran off. With all my "Gilligan Hitches" coming loose and the stud going full bore, pretty soon the deer was on the very end of thirty feet of lariat and only hitting the ground and the tops of big sagebrush every now and then.

It was about two miles to the Drift Fence Gate and I'd closed it when I came through. Now, I'm running behind the rapidly disappearing dust storm on a trail of uprooted brush, deer hide and pieces of deer meat with tears running down my cheeks.

The stud stopped at the gate without crashing through it, which was lucky considering what had transpired in the recent past.

When I got up to him, the rope was still dragging. On the end were two hind leg bones about 1 foot long with <u>no</u> meat and very little hide left.

Needless to say, the rest of the trip home to what I had visualized as a hero's welcome to the mighty hunter's return became a quest for what to tell them. Ultimately, I opted for the truth – as hard as it was to 'fess up.

Here are a couple of the other memorable horse lashups of my early years. (There will be many more before this novella ends!)

We had somehow ended up with an old Thoroughbred race horse that had been blinded in the left eye, hence the moniker "Deadeye."

The highway (now Highway 93) through the valley had been a dirt road but was being widened and oiled. It was about 100 yards from our kitchen window. The cottonwood trees in the borrow pit had been sawed off just above ground level.

One morning we were having breakfast when someone looked out and saw some of our range cows coming by headed up the highway. Dad said to me, "Saddle Deadeye and bring those cattle back." I ran to the corral, saddled and bridled, and headed after the cattle.

Now, it was late fall and plenty cold, and I had on a pair of heavy gloves. Deadeye loved to run, but he was cold jawed. When I went by the cows, he wouldn't stop and just kept running. Not wanting to keep going 'til he ran himself down, I came up with a plan. (One of many that resulted in a similar fashion.) I decided if I took my gloves off and leaned up on his neck with my right arm over it I could drop my weight down and sort of bulldog him to a stop.

Now, there was no witness to this, but I can tell you it worked! I led him around, settled him down, put my gloves back on (it was cold!), and got back on to head back toward the ranch. Would you believe it – he ran away again, and we went by the cows going the other way!

This time, I had a mental lapse and an audience. I forgot to take the gloves off and in a very short time of hanging on to his neck and head my hands started to slip. I was basically upside down under his neck and shoulders looking down at the tree stumps going by at the speed of a runaway Thoroughbred with my grip losing friction with every jump. I didn't know it for a while, but I was right in front of the house with everyone watching, when the hands came loose. I hit upside down into the stumps, rocks and gravel, and Deadeye ran on over me as I flipped and bounced to a stop.

I don't remember who caught Deadeye or got the cows in, as I was sort of, like, out of it.

The next chapter of the "Deadeye Saga" went like this:

I had gotten the idea to try to be a cowboy, as in "Rodeo Cowboy." Deadeye could catch any calf in just a few jumps, so it was just a matter of a little training and practice and we would be ready.

I'd watched the big boys (real calf ropers) and studied how they rigged their gear. I'd seen the neck ropes to keep the horses head pointed toward the calf. So, I built me a neck rope, run my lariat through it and back to the horn, and we were off in search of an unsuspecting calf.

I found some cows and calves out in the North 40, lined one out and roped him. (I'd already been practicing on the dogs, cats, chickens, etc.)

I got Deadeye stopped okay, because I'd gotten a little harsher bit for him, and I got off to tie the calf. He ran around Deadeye; Deadeye spooked and ran away with the calf. My neck rope was too big and allowed the rope to be nearly back to the saddle horn, defeating the purpose.

Anyway, big runaway around the end of a fence line with the calf's head on one side of the gate post and horse and rope on the other at the speed of a runaway race horse, again.

When I got there in five minutes or so, the poor calf appeared dead – eyes rolled back until I couldn't see the pupils, and the broken rope with the hondo and a couple inches of rope around his neck. Once again, I'm following the horse tracks and the dragging rope when here comes Dad on a dead run. The horse and broken rope had ended up at the corral.

We went back and the calf was coming to and made it okay.

Stan Potts receiving trophies at the National High School Rodeo in Augusta, Montana, in 1952. His finishes were second in average for bulldogging, third in bareback riding, a tie for runner-up with Alvin Nelson at 200 points in the accumulated average category.

Chapter 5

National High School Rodeo 1952

I kept on practicing my calf roping and started riding bareback broncs and also steer wrestling. I went to a lot of the nearby amateur rodeos in Idaho, Nevada and Montana, and I received an invitation to the first ever Idaho Cowboys Association Finals Rodeo in American Falls, Idaho.

I was invited in bareback, calf roping and bulldogging, and I placed three or four times in the go-rounds but didn't do very well overall.

I had graduated from high school in Mackay, Idaho, in the spring of 1952. While rodeoing that summer, I saw a poster about the National High School Rodeo to be held in Augusta, Montana, that fall. I knew nothing about it but called to find out the details. They said the association was formed in Halletsville, Texas, in 1947, and state associations were slowly being formed.

They told me that I would be eligible by doing the following because Idaho did not have a high school rodeo association: 1) a letter from my school principal that I had passing grades; and 2) three letters from rodeo committees that I had competed at and three pictures, one from each of the events I wanted to enter.

I got all my stuff in, and along with Jerry Twitchell of Mackay in the saddle bronc riding and Stanley Allen from Salmon in bulldogging, we became the first cowboys from Idaho to ever attend a National High School Rodeo Finals. The state formed an association in the following years and since has sent lots of cowboys and cowgirls.

Anyway, Dad had bought a new, blue Chevy pickup and let me take it. We took our sleeping bags and slept in the Augusta High School gymnasium. Of course, I didn't have any horses and hoped I could get mounted in the dogging and roping.

The kid from Salmon had a dogging horse that his dad had won in a claiming race. He let me use Popeye, and that was a great piece of luck for Popeye was a natural. For the next several years, he probably was one of the two or three best dogging horses in the Northwest. Danny Gorrell from Gooding bought him, and I was lucky enough to mount him at several later rodeos.

I didn't know anybody for a hazer and got one of the guys that was helping put on the rodeo to haze for me. He didn't know <u>anything</u> about hazing, and I didn't know very much about bulldogging. In fact, I had thrown so few steers that I decided to practice by grabbing one out of the bunch in the steer pen. I had on a pretty white shirt and a pair of sunglasses when I grabbed the steer by the horns.

Total chaos followed! I had no idea those steers could be so protective of one another. By the time I figured out how to turn him loose, his buddies had trampled, kicked, hooked and crapped all over this Idaho kid! My shirt was torn, glasses were broke, and there was a grass green tint to what was left of my clothes.

Anyway, my first steer came out and I happened to be just right on the score, but the hazer was still in the box and the steer faded away. I got pulled back on and took him after a lap or so around the arena. Time was sixty seconds. Not what I'd planned.

My next steer (I'd found a hazer) I bulldogged in six seconds flat, the fastest steer of the rodeo. This let me make the finals, and I was 11 on my last steer, three in seventy-seven seconds. <u>But</u> I won second in the average

At Mackay, Idaho, in 1952.

and with my go-round times it was worth 130 points toward the all-around.

In the bareback riding, I made two fair rides on my first two, won a third and a fourth and made the finals in the bareback. I drew one of Zumwalt's best bareback horses for my final horse. Bad luck again. The same guy that had tried to haze for me on my first steer was opening the gate.

My horse started bucking in the chute before I was set, and he opened the gate. I tried to hold the horse in with my foot, but it got out. Zumwalt would not let me have that horse back as it had bucked empty across the arena.

My re-ride was a very small horse, and I didn't get him started. No score on my final horse. Judge Billy Lawrence goose-egged me. But I won third in the average on two horses. Seventy more points.

In the calf roping, I tied my first one in eighteen seconds; my second in sixteen seconds. The kids from the South were tying them in eleven and twelve, especially one kid from Waxahatche, Texas, named Poochie Appelt. Hereafter, came my worst mistake – I decided I'd have to catch fast and would only pack one rope. I missed my calf, but so did Poochie and several of the other speed balls. If I had have carried two loops and caught my second I might have still placed fairly good in the average and might have won the all-around saddle.

Frank Anderson, hazer, and Stan Potts, dogger, in competition.

Rigging over the head – not good. At Spokane, Washington, in 1953.

As it was, I tied for second with Alvin Nelson and was twenty points out of first place for the National High School All-Around title. I never did like to lose, but with a few mistakes that had been made that loss was especially hard. All-Around Champion was Franklin Menke of Edgemont, South Dakota.

Alvin Nelson went on to be world champion saddle bronc rider a couple of years later and held the title for several years.

Of course, the present day high school champions are several cuts above where we were in 1952. My times and scores would probably not have gained me a point in recent years; however, I was one of the first and very proud of what I was able to do.

I went to college at the University of Idaho that fall and was lucky enough to win the all-around at one of the rodeos. I won the calf roping and bareback riding at Kennewick, Washington, on Mother's Day, 1953. The all-around saddle is engraved "Pacific Coast Conference – All-Around Cowboy 1953." I have given it to my oldest grandson, Jay Black.

After we moved to Nevada, I rodeoed for three or four years and was lucky enough to win the Nevada State Bulldogging Championship in 1958 and 1960 and was runner-up for the all-around, bull riding and bareback riding a couple of times.

My bulldogging luck had a lot to do with the horse I mostly used. Dean Oliver had a sorrel calf roping mare named Brandy that he won the Idaho state amateur championship several times on. In 1954, when he went professional, he got a new horse because Brandy wouldn't work the rope good. Harry Charters bought Brandy from Dean and converted her to a dogging horse. She was a natural and loved it. When Harry joined the RCA in about 1957, he bought a race horse named Buddy Bill, and I was able to get Brandy from him.

Someone shot her through the cannon bone with a .22 while she was in the pasture, and we had to destroy her – Sad Day.

A saddle bronc ride in 1952. Note the daylight.

Gordon Wines presents Stan Potts with a bulldogging saddle and buckle from Cactus Pete's in 1958 for the Nevada Cowboys Association championship..

*A COLLECTION OF STAN POTTS'
RODEO PHOTOGRAPHS*

Author's Note: Felix Cooper helped me fight bulls at Mackay about 1955. He was shining shoes at the Bonneville Hotel in Idaho Falls when I met him. Here's an interesting story about him.

WAY BACK WHEN

Felix Cooper relives the good old rodeo days

■ By TEDDY ALLEN
SPECIAL TO THE PSN

Billy Upshaw photo

Arthritis and bulls and stubborn saddle broncs have finally caught up with Felix Cooper.

His family at his home in tiny Pelican, La., is gone. And so are his skills that, between 1934-66, made him one of the most versatile cowboys and bullfighters in what is now known as the Professional Rodeo Cowboys Association.

"Bareback, saddle bronc and bull riding, he was capable of winning them all," said Harry Tompkins of Dublin, Texas, winner of eight world championships including two all-around titles. "I never heard Felix cuss anybody, never saw him drunk, out of line . . . I never heard him complain.

"And I've hardly ever seen him bucked off."

Cooper later performed as a rodeo clown. He is proud of the fact that no fallen rider was ever injured by a bull while he was in the arena.

"You had to always be in shape and be really quick and fast," said Cooper, who retired from clowning in 1966. "Good showmanship was expected and I tried to give it to the people."

Those days are dust now. Now he rides a wheelchair, a concession to 80 years and a way of life that begged for bumps and bruises.

In a voice soft but filled with life and personality, Cooper still flavors the stories from his rodeo career with smiles at the Mansfield Nursing Center in Mansfield, La., where he's lived since February, 1991.

"The life was good; it was a social affair," Cooper said of riding the circuit, his once-strong hands curled on the lap of his overalls, a straw cowboy

—40—

hat covering most of his gray-speckled hair. "All the cowboys were friendly. They were just regular people, great people."

The arena will never be loud again for Cooper, once a 5-feet-9, 168-pound bundle of tightly-wound cowboy. But the memories remain fresh. Strong. And happy. It doesn't seem to bother Cooper that, as a young black cowboy more than 50 years ago, he had to battle prejudice as well as salty stock.

"They didn't give the black rider what he had coming," Tompkins said. "If he was supposed to win first, he'd be lucky to win fourth."

In Cooper's case, the prejudice may have had as much to do with jealousy as with the color of his skin.

"Of all the black cowboys I knew in my time from 1948 until now, Felix Cooper was the best rider," Tompkins said. "He could beat anybody, anytime!"

"It didn't make me feel happy," Cooper said about the times prejudice cost him a buckle. "But that was no need to make a show. You just go up to a fella and tell him what you mean."

Felix Cooper, 80, treasures the old photos from his days as a roughstock cowboy and bullfighter. Cooper, whose rodeo career spanned more than 30 years, now resides in a nursing home in Mansfield, La. He still loves to tell stories of his days on the professional rodeo circuit.

Cooper leans forward, as if he were talking to a rodeo judge behind the chutes 50 years ago and says, "I think you did me wrong, man. I know these other guys can ride, but, hey, I can ride, too."

But didn't Cooper ever want more? More buckles? Less cheating?

What about the time in Calgary, when the judges goose-egged him when he fell off the bronc he was riding because another horse running free in the arena ran into his horse?

"How'd I handle it?" Cooper said.

"Well, I wouldn't handle it. I'd go on to the next town."

But didn't prejudice wait there, too? What about the time in Salt Lake City, when he placed second after riding a bull so mean he was shipped from Texas in a boxcar by himself?

"I just went on the to the next town," Cooper said.

Those towns included St. Louis, Chicago, Philadelphia, Denver and New York City.

Cooper just kept going, looking for eight seconds on a bull's back and ignoring the long trips, hard times, meals of raisin bread, cheap motels and cheap shots from cowboys who couldn't ride as well as he could.

He had the fever since he rode the wire fence outside his home as a boy. He'd get thrown and get cut and get well and get on again. Or he'd run barefoot through the pasture and jump on a bull's back to "just to try to ride him," he said.

He didn't even know how good he was at age 17, when he signed on with a Wild West Show in 1929, five years before his first pro rodeo.

"I found out all stock was the same," he said. "I could ride 'em."

Their names were Hell's Angel, Sidecar and Headhunter. And he could ride them all.

He still does. Age doesn't take the cowboy out of the soul. In many ways, he's still a kid bouncing on his older cousin's knee 80 years ago in Pelican.

"All I ever wanted to be since then," he said, "was a cowboy."

Reprinted by permission of The Times *in Shreveport, La.*

DeVere Helfrich photo

Here, Felix Cooper fights a bull at the 1954 Red Bluff Round-up Rodeo in Red Bluff, California. He is proud of the fact that no bull rider ever was injured while he worked the arena as a bullfighter. Cooper was injured in the area only once in his 32-year professional rodeo career.

Chapter 6

The Houston Place

Along through the mid-1940s, my dad leased some farms in the Lost River Valley. Although I wasn't very big, I could help him quite a bit. I could drive teams on all the equipment, plus we got our first tractor about then. It was an 8N Ford with mower, plow and blade for a cost of $800 brand new. Naturally, I learned to drive it right off.

When I was about twelve, Dad asked me if I wanted to go partners to buy one of the ranches he'd been leasing. It belonged to an older couple who lived at Firth, Idaho, and they were too far away to take care of it. The price was $12,000 for 117 acres with an old abandoned log house that we were using for a granary. He said he would put up the $2,000 down – we would run it each year, make the payment of $1,000 plus 3% interest, and split what was left. Typical ranching dream! I don't remember any money ever being left, but we were improving the fences, killing the quack grass, and generally getting it to produce better.

When Joy and I got married in 1954, Dad and Mom gave us their half of the ranch for a wedding present. Joy's Dad and Mom told us to bring the stock truck to Nevada, and they would load it with cattle. They gave us a two-year-old bull and nine heifers.

We fixed the old house up a little and moved in. The wind blew through the logs, and we nearly froze to death the first winter. There was no well, so we had to pack water about 200 yards from the creek. There was an outhouse, and my Grandmother Gray lived with us one winter. We had to help her out and back as she was getting pretty frail by then. A neighbor helped me hand dig a well, probably 20 feet. We got a tiny bit of water – enough to put a pump on it, and by being ultraconservative we made it work.

We basically did everything to try and survive. I worked out whenever I could find a job – mostly in the mines at Wildhorse and Cobalt.

Pigs

We bought a Duroc sow and twelve baby pigs (the first money I ever borrowed from a bank – $180). We had good luck, mostly grazed them out and planned on making some good money. There were six gilts and six barrows. When we hauled them to Mackay to sell, we found out the price was the lowest it had ever been – 10 cents a pound. We naturally had to sell the barrows but decided to keep the gilts, breed them and make it big that way. Hah! Once more, good luck on *that* part of the plan to raise a lot of hogs – good litters, low death rate, good gain, etc, but that was about the end of the good luck.

First, we had a spring flood. With a foot of snow, the ground was frozen, and in came a Chinook wind with warm rain. There were no high places on this ranch, so pretty quick the hogs were swimming around the barnyard. We were able to get them on top of a baled hay stack, about three or four bales high, and saved most of them.

Next, we were gone one day, and when Joy came home the hogs had rooted the door open, and some of them were in the house. We had started square dancing, and I had bought Joy this beautiful turquoise and brown square dance dress. Guess what the hogs ruined!

And, then, Joy had gone to the barn to milk the cow and do chores. I was gone for a week working at the mine in Wildhorse. She got between one of the sows and her litter, and the sow charged. Joy hit the sow with buckets of milk and climbed the fence. Next, she called the hog buyer and sold out – all of them – so when I came home from the mine I was no longer in the hog business. Oh, we finally got the rest of the $180 paid to the bank!

Sheep

Next, we decided to try the sheep raising game. I went to Cokeville, Wyo., bought 300 broken mouth ewes (six-year-olds mostly). The plan was to breed them, winter them, lamb them out, and sell the pairs in the spring. Some neighbors had been doing this and were really doing good – $60 to $80 a pair.

I paid $10 a head for the ewes and 53 cents each to get them to Leslie on the railroad. I trailed them home from there. A few days after I got them home, a neighbor from above the reservoir, Vic Johnson, came by and asked if I wanted to sell part of them. Ultimately we sold him his choice of 200 head for $16 apiece. That left me with 100 all paid for, but, naturally, they were the 100 worst ones. We went ahead and bred them and ended up with a pretty good lamb crop and low death loss. We're finally going to make a little money, right? Wrong!

Nobody wanted to buy any sheep that spring! I finally dropped the price to $20 a pair – no takers. I ended up hauling them to Salmon and putting them through Mike Isley's auction. They brought $17 a pair. It might have paid for the hay but not the lambing shed that the wind rolled into the creek, or the labor for us getting up every couple of hours all night long while lambing.

Horses

I broke a lot of horses during this period, also. I built a nice round corral, and people brought colts from all around. I would ride them for two weeks for $50. Basically, I got them so the owner could get on and go ahead with them.

Finally, I was getting more colts than I could handle. I had read this story by an old horse trainer from Ely, Nevada, named Wiley Carroll. It was how to take care of and train several colts at one time.

The theory method was as follows: Say you have six unbroken horses that all need training to lead, to saddle, to rein, etc. His method was to get a saddle on one, then head and tail the rest of the group behind him. You get on him and he can't get away because the ones behind him pull back because they don't know how to lead, but they are learning.

After you get some time on the first one, you unsaddle him, saddle the second one, put the first one on the back end, and then start over.

I can report with authority that it will work – if you don't get killed in the process. And I also learned you need lots of open space – no barbed wire fences.

Here are a couple of the individual horses I worked with that both did the same thing – definitely not what you would expect.

We were living at Mackay, and a sheepman from the head of the Lost River, Bert Coates, brought me a big, brown five-year-old gelding. This horse had a very unique start in life! The winter of 1949-50 was a tough one. Bert, as well as a lot of other ranchers, ran their horses on the range summer and winter, only gathering horses as they needed them – teams for haying, stock for roundup, etc.

About March or April, he went to gather and found dead horses all over. Some were still alive but nearly starved. He said he saw something that he thought was an eagle eating on a dead horse. He rode up, and here was this colt nursing on its dead mother's ears. He brought it back to the ranch. It survived and was turned back out as a yearling. It hadn't been in the gather again until he brought him to me.

I started him, and he was a very intelligent horse. I probably had seven or eight rides on him when I got hurt in a bulldogging accident – ran a steer horn through my left hip and was out of commission for several days.

I was supposed to have this horse ready for pickup but was running out of time. I needed to hurry the process all I could, so when I healed up enough to get on him I decided to take a long circle to see if I could catch up on the training.

I was up in the mountains and started up a fairly steep hill. He didn't want to go and kept turning back downhill. I worked him over, and he started bucking down through a rock pile, got me loose and off, jerked the reins away and took off for home.

He probably went a quarter mile, stopped, looked back at me, and came trotting back. He let me catch him, and off we went. The training process was working. I didn't try to go back straight up the hill!

I got him finished with no more problems, and as far as I know he went on to be a good mount.

The second one was a black colt we had raised out of our Quarter Horse herd. He had one white eye, and we called him Popeye. He was a big three-year-old when I got around to starting him one spring. He was super-intelligent. He learned to lead on a slack rope the second day, and took to the saddle and bit like he couldn't wait to learn it all!

After we got out of the corral, he loved to lope figure eights, practice stops – everything about the process. He loved it so much that by the third or fourth ride he would come across the corral and meet me at the gate to be caught and saddled. Then, I became terribly busy with the spring work.

He'd come to the gate and wait for me, and I'd have to walk on by to some ranch crisis or at least a perceived crisis. Probably a couple of weeks went by before I could get back to him.

He did not come to the gate, didn't come to be caught, would not look at me, and when we went out of the corral, he would not try to learn anything. He was spooky and tried to buck. I decided to take him up on Clover Mountain and burn some energy out of him. After an hour or two of neither one of us learning anything, he whirled and started bucking down through the cedar and pinion trees. He landed out into the top branches of a big cedar, and as we crashed down through it I came unglued (as in fell off!).

He went right down past the ranch house and corrals and headed toward the railroad track at a dead run. I walked in, got the Jeep and headed after him. I got around him, headed him back and several of the neighbors helped me get him in the corral. I went to the house and got my bareback spurs (deciding that we had to have it out right then).

With far too much of an audience, I got on him, put the spurs to him, and for a couple minutes nearly had the upper hand. Then, my left bridle rein broke, and he bucked me off again. From that point forward he seemed to know, and I guess I did to, that he could buck me off at will.

A few days after this I was trailing the horse herd to our field at Tobar. I was riding Popeye, and I could tell he was going to try me again. There was a deep snowdrift along the fence, and when he broke in two and started bucking, I reined him into the deep snow to give me all the advantage I could get. He bucked me off again in three feet of snow and took off after the horse herd now about a half mile ahead and on a trot.

He went part way after them, stopped, looked back at me, turned and trotted back – stopping about twenty feet away. I walked up, got on and from then on we both knew who had the upper hand.

I asked a cowboy friend of mine, Boyd Tripp, if he could take him. Boyd was buckarooing for The Marble Ranch and could put lots of miles on him. He bucked Boyd off several times that summer, so we decided to make a bucking horse out of him. However, he would never buck as hard when we wanted him to. So, through my fault, a potential great horse became a nothing.

Why these horses came back to me after being loose and free, I do not know.

Crops

While we were still at the farm at Mackay, we tried several different crops. Field seed peas were one that worked pretty good, but we could only get a few acre contract each year.

Potatoes were another story. The first year we planted, we borrowed all the equipment and planted five acres. It was a dream come true. They were worth $8 per hundred, and we cleared over $1,000 per acre.

So, with typical Potts abandon we bought some equipment and headed out to get rich in the spud business. We raised a super crop – had over 10,000 sacks of number ones in the cellar, plus nearly that many sacks of seed, all certified. You couldn't give them away, although we finally did. We sold the whole cellar full for twenty cents per hundred – and the check bounced!

We had sold the farm that winter to Orville and Lloyd Smith for $18,600 cash, so we paid our bills, the last $2,000 on the ranch, and went to Nevada to help Joy's folks feed the cattle that winter. We had $10,000 left after the sale and clearing our bills.

This picture was taken a year after we bought the Nevada ranch. From left to right are Stan Potts, his brother Don Gray, Dottie Gray and Joy Potts. Kay Potts is in front.

Chapter 7

Cattle Hunt at the Atomic Energy Commission

While we were ranching at Mackay I had a unique experience out in the desert between Arco and American Falls.

The Atomic Energy Commission (AEC) had built a large experimental facility there to test atomic-powered engines for submarines. The facility, which is now called the Idaho National Engineering Environmental Laboratory or INEEL (primarily to get away from the negative words of "atomic energy"), covered probably twenty miles of desert, and the highway to Blackfoot passed through the area. All roads into the area were posted with guards.

My neighbor, Hoot Anderson, was a livestock hauler and took cattle from Mackay to Blackfoot in his truck. One night, about midnight, the phone rang and it was Hoot. He had tipped a load of cattle over in the middle of the AEC, and they were headed through the area. The insurance company needed me to try and round them up or at least get them away from the complex.

I saddled and trailered a horse and met Hoot and some of the guards from the AEC. They took us to where the wreck was, and I started out on the cattle tracks. They had bunched up and headed south, pretty much in a straight line, to just a couple miles east of the Big Butte.

I crossed the railroad track that connected Blackfoot to the Lost River Valley and followed the cattle tracks until I could see the valley toward American Falls. I was sure we were off the AEC lands and headed back, not knowing all the excitement I had caused.

It seems that off somewhere in the direction I had headed was the dump site for the radioactive waste. After I had been gone several hours someone realized this, and then the search was on for me.

I got about three miles from the highway and saw red lights, blue lights, dust and vehicles tearing around. One of them spotted me and came to send me back.

After they explained it to me I had visions of a pond of atomic waste just laying out in the desert. Then one of them told me it had a ten-foot-high chain link and electric fence around it!

One of the guards had this reflection on the day's excitement: "We have been practicing all kinds of scenarios, like an invasion by the Russians, and here we can't even figure out what to do with one guy on a saddle horse. We have torn up several vehicles, and the guy comes riding back not even knowing we were looking for him!"

Chapter 8

The Angel Creek Ranch
(The Bues Place, Warren Angel Creek Ranch, The Jimmy Ralph Place, The Pio Aguirre Place, The Arascada Place And Finally They Called It The Potts Place!)

On our way to help Joy's folks at their Lamoille, Nevada, ranch, we stopped to look at a ranch that was for sale in Clover Valley, just south of Wells, Nevada. I had been on the ranch before; an old Basque cowboy named Pio Aguirre would invite us broke cowboys to come out and sleep during the Wells rodeo every spring.

The ranch was 1,520 acres with an old two-story, ten-room, six-bedroom, house. There were ninety-six cows, four bulls, six horses, a couple of tractors, miles of falling down fence, and a lease on 1,440 acres of pasture at Tobar about ten miles down the valley.

We actually bought the ranch on our way to Joy's folks, so we never did make it to help them. I was never one to spend a long time making up my mind on something. It was never always right, but at least I was speedy!

We gave owner Marge Arascada $5,000, and we took over a mortgage of $49,500. Her husband, Pete, had worked himself to death, they said. I should have heeded that.

We unloaded our Quarter Horse stud, our old cat Josephine, four baby kittens, a half-grown cat named Joe Little, then headed back to Idaho for the rest of our Quarter Horse mares, truck, pickup, furniture, etc.

Quarter Horses

A little word about the Quarter Horses. When I was in high school, I had gone to a Quarter Horse sale at the Mackay rodeo grounds. It was a dispersal sale of Boyd Gibbs' horses. I had saved a little money from my 4-H projects, so I was a potential buyer if prices seemed right. Not very far into the sale I could tell that before it was over I would probably buy something. There was a sorrel mare by Chief McCue named Chief Delight with a stud colt by Orange Ade and rebred to Gibbs' new stallion, Johnnie Dawson, that came through. I bought the package for $165. I should have spent every cent I had there as that $165 investment made me over $20,000 in the next ten years, and I missed the Big One!

I kept rebreeding Chief Delight to Johnnie Dawson. I sold one of the colts when he was a weanling for $400 to a pair of race horse men from Blackfoot named Hillman and Brown. I didn't know it, but they entered him in the Intermountain Quarter Horse Futurity. In September of 1958, the year we bought the ranch in Clover Valley, I received a phone call from Hillman and Brown. They said, "Guess what, your colt won the futurity for $28,000!"

Anyway, we had a few of the horses including Chief Delight's last colt, a palomino stud named Kenny Dawson and several young mares. It seemed when things would go bad on the ranch we could find a buyer for a horse. Ultimately they were all gone as things always found ways to go bad.

Best Laid Plans

My plans were to use the $5,000 we had left from our ranch sale in Mackay to operate the first year or two in Clover Valley (back then, you

Stan Potts and "Goucho" about the time we roped the bobcat!

actually could with $5,000). Then, I would trade the steer calves for heifers, breed them, and sell the couple hundred cows to clear the mortgage. Then I would go to work for someone else and buy cows back a few at a time to restock the ranch. By selling pasture and hay, I figured I could restock it within ten years and never have it in debt again. The tax situation back then would allow it.

Ah, the best laid plans.

Nevada went into a four-year drought a few months after we bought the ranch. Pretty quick, the $5,000 was gone buying feed for the cattle. I was hauling hay clear from Little Lost River in Idaho, only because I had bought it for $12 a ton. While I was hauling it, it was worth $50 or $60 a ton, but I couldn't sell it as I needed it to keep my cows alive. I could make three truck loads per week but barely kept the cattle fed.

I would haul a load of cows to Twin Falls, sell them, and buy hay for the rest of the cows with the money. Oh, well!

A bit of levity in the situation – Joy and I went to Tremonton, Utah, to talk to the people who owned the 1,440 acres at Tobar. He was a district court judge named B.C. Call. I really went over there to talk about the lease, but Mr. Call said, "Why don't you just buy it from me? I'll take $9 per acre with $2,000 down."

Plowing the garden in Nevada.

Well, snap decisions again – I wrote him a check for $2,000, knowing I could get the money to cover it somewhere.

As soon as I got home, I went to the bank and told my banker I needed $2,000. All I had was a checking account then, no loan history, so the banker, Charlie Ballew, asked for the name of my banker in Mackay as a reference and told me to come back the next day.

I walked in and he had a rather pained look on his face. His words: "Quite a reference you gave me. Your banker just embezzled $100,000 from the Mackay bank!" My heart sank – but he loaned us the money.

I felt I just needed it for short time 'til I could negotiate a loan with Mr. Helth who held the note on the home place. When I told him what I'd done, he said, "Hell, that ground isn't worth $5 an acre." But, he went ahead and added it to the existing note with the 1,440 acres as security.

I could see things weren't going to hold together very long the way things were working, so we put the ranch up for sale with the hopes of salvaging something.

We sold it all to a hotshot developer from Los Angeles named K.B. Kiker for $5,000 down and great promises for the rest.

We moved to town, and I went to work for International Construction Co. building microwave towers across northeastern Nevada.

Kiker moved about twenty hired men into the house, started tearing

"Pete" the bobcat we raised in Nevada.

down fences, planting grain, and hauling in semi-load after semi-load of sprinkler pipe, equipment, pumps, etc. It looked like a going deal, except the growing season is not that long and most of the grain crops were going in during June and July. Naturally, the crops froze before they were ripe, and my payments weren't coming in. After repeated phone calls, I was able to talk to Mr. Kiker. He said his wife was divorcing him and she was getting a $2 million settlement. He was going to give up most of his projects across Nevada but wanted to keep our place. He asked, "Would you be interested in trading for one of my four motels across the street from Disneyland?"

I told him I'd have to come down and see them, but I didn't have any money. He said to find out the airfare for me, Joy and the three girls and he'd send me the money. It was $500. He sent it, and we got in our little Chevy II station wagon and drove down. He put us up in one of the motels called the "Pixie." It was between two orange groves with one of the entrances to Disneyland right across the street. It had 98 units. Anyway, we looked at them all and decided against doing it (primarily because we didn't want to raise the girls in Los Angeles). The Convention Center was built on one of the orange groves within the next few years, so we could have sold out and made a bundle.

Joy and the girls drove home, and Kiker sent his pilot, Art Starbuck, with one of his airplanes to take me to Mexico fishing. He really was trying to figure out how to salvage the ranch. He gave us about $20,000 more, hired me to run it the next year, but folded up in mid-year. I filed a lien for my wages, foreclosed on the ranch, and a year later we got it back.

I could see that the sprinklers were the answer to irrigating rocky, uneven ground, and we were able to get some pretty good deals on pipe, pumps, engines, etc., and went ahead with the development.

The bad thing was that I worked my family so hard on it for the next few years. With a swather, rake, two balers and a harobed bale wagon, the three girls, Kay's friend "Debby the Baler" from California, and I put up all the hay. Everybody was kind of burnt out on it, and we decided to sell it again. Joy and I took over managing the ranch for the next five years.

The year we bought the ranch we cut about 100 ton of weeds, slough grass and rabbit brush. The year we sold the ranch, successfully, we cut about 1,800 ton of good alfalfa-grass hay.

During the development of the ranch, we had to drill some wells. Part of the irrigation, about 240 acres, was a gravity system from Angel Creek that a neighbor, Russ Peavey, loaned us the money to put in. We shut off a couple of 471 GMC (Jimmy) diesel pumps that burned a couple hundred gallons of diesel a day. The day we shut them off and turned the water into the twelve-inch pipeline was a happy day in Pottsville! We paid Mr. Peavey back on the pipeline in four years!

The wells were somewhat of a different deal. The first two I tried turned out to be 200-foot holes in the dust. My nickname in Nevada was "Dry Hole!"

Frank Riggle and "The Theory of Mass Attraction"

Then an old guy came by one day, prospecting. His name was Frank Riggle. He said he could find the water for me. I asked him how, and he said, "By 'The Theory of Mass Attraction.'" Well, here we are walking all over my ranch – an old guy with an Alka Seltzer® bottle full of water in the end of a plastic bread sack, swinging it back and forth in an arc about a foot off the ground, and a younger old guy trailing along behind (and hoping the neighbors aren't watching!).

Anyway, two different spots he picked were somewhere in the vicinity of where I needed water. Another was only about thirty feet from where I had a well that pumped 800 gallons per minute. He said, "Too bad you didn't drill here. You would have had a 3,000 g.p.m. well!"

I drilled one of the other spots he picked and got about what he said, 600 g.p.m. at about the depth he said, 120 feet.

Mr. Riggle was one of life's characters. He had done everything worth doing and some things that weren't. He would go on for hours with some story that you knew was just that. Then he'd totter out to his pickup and come back with the scrapbook of pictures of his Irish Setter bitch nursing a fawn deer or of him bulldogging a bull elk!

He had been in charge of the horseshoers at Ft. Keogh, Montana, during the cavalry days – 18,000 horses and 300 horseshoers and proof of it also!

He had put in a full career with the U.S. Forest Service in the early days of Yellowstone Park.

He hired me and my airplane to fly him around the West prospecting for gold. No, we didn't land – we prospected in the air. Yup, the plastic bag and the Alka Seltzer bottle, only this time it was full of gold dust and nuggets!

Okay, the Theory of Mass Attraction: I have no idea, but he said that all matter attracts like matter. His ability to evidently sense a difference in the gravitational pull of a small amount of matter (in the Alka Seltzer bottle) to an underground channel or body of water or a body of gold-bearing ore was what he used.

He showed me clippings of stories about a big gold strike in South

America that he claimed to have located for a mining company that hired him at a wage of $1,000 a day for thirty days. Who knows – I damn sure wasn't going to question him after all the other things he'd proven to have done!

Three or four years later, I decided to drill another well and got Farnes Egbert, a Mormon bishop and rancher friend from Metropolis, to come "witch" it.

He used the green willow method to locate the water and a bent baling wire to estimate depth and volume. After a day of walking the ranch, he picked the same spot Frank had picked a few years earlier, with the same estimate of depth and volume.

Where do you think I drilled? Right there, you bet, and it was the best well we had on the ranch – about 1,200 g.p.m. at sixty-five foot lift.

Whatever it is that those people have, it's far better than the Potts Dry Hole System.

The family during the time we were ranching in Nevada. From left are Robyn, Stani, Joy, Stan and Kay Potts.

Chapter 9

More Experiences While We Lived in Nevada

We spent a total of twenty years at the ranch in Nevada. Our girls Kay, Robyn and Stani were raised and went to school there until Stani, the youngest, was a senior in high school. She attended Twin Falls High, but came back to Wells to graduate with the class she had started kindergarten with.

In the course of trying to make the ranch work, we bought a range permit in the desert valley east and south of the ranch. We were able to run about three hundred head and would bring the cattle back to the ranch in the fall. Had a few good years (broke even) and one where we actually made some money.

We had a 1953 Cessna 180 (2242 C), and I had a little road in the hayfield that I used for a strip. I would fly about one-half hour morning and evening and could keep track of water holes, windmills, and cattle rustlers, etc. Real easy cowboying. (While I was doing this kind of flying, I got pretty proficient at short field take offs and landings as my Jeep trail through the alfalfa field was only about 600 feet long and over a barbed wire fence and up to the highway and power line). One year we were pasturing off the aftermath of the hay and grain fields and had the nightmare of bloating twenty head of real nice two-year-old Hereford heifers. I didn't have any place to go with the rest of the cattle so called a cow buyer and sold the rest at fire sale prices, put the 1,440 acre place and the range permit together for sale. We were able to sell it to a neighbor and never tried to run cattle again.

I'd always wanted to learn to fly. I'd had three airplane rides before I was six years old. When I was at the University of Idaho, they had a flying club. It cost $50 to join and $4 an hour to fly. I could never come up with an extra $50 to join but flew with some of my buddies that were members.

When we moved to Nevada, several of us started a flying club and bought a 1947 Aeronca Champ for $1,100. One of the local pilots,

Ken Jewkes, had a license called a Limited Flight Instructor (LFI). He could teach you, but then you had to fly with a certified flight instructor. That's when I was able to start flying in 1958. Joy buckarooed for the neighbors to pay my way into the flying club.

Joy's parents, Lloyd and Marion Blume, had a hunting camp at Lamoille, Nevada. Because we had quite a few horses, Joy's Dad said we should try to get a packer's license and take some deer hunters each fall. He helped us go to Dr. Harry Gallagher, the chairman of the Elko County Big Game Management Board, and get a packer and guide license for the east side of the Humboldt Mountains, the Wood Hills, Spruce Mountain, and the Pequop Mountains. We ran an ad in the *San Francisco Examiner* for four-day deer hunts at $100 per person. They stayed at the house. Joy fed them, and I would take them hunting. The quota was two bucks and one doe and most people got all three, so I packed a lot of deer off the mountain. One year, sixty-eight, I remember. Some of the deer were really nice with the best ones a thirty-four inch four pointer taken by Harry Robinson and a thirty-seven inch non-typical taken by Olie Forquer. We got some lion dogs and took lion hunters also. The first Nevada trophy record book had two of the top five until that time taken by us, with Ken Johnson's lion winning an award at the Boone & Crockett Convention in Denver, Colorado, with

Olie Forquer and his 37inch buck.

a score of 15 5/16.

One night I got a call from the local Chief of Police wondering if I could fly him and a couple of drug enforcement agents on an attempted drug bust the next morning. I told him yes and I would meet them at the Wells Airport the next morning. We headed south and they filled me in on what we were going to try to do. An informant had told them that a DC-3 loaded with marijuana would be landing at a dry lake-bed near the southern Utah-Nevada border. They had a map, the radio frequencies, pass words, time schedule, etc. Another group of agents was to apprehend the pickup vehicles (two reinforced heavy-duty vans where they left the highway south of Pioche). We would take over their code passwords and tell the DC-3 to go ahead and land and unload and the vans were on the way but would be a little late. We got within a few miles, staying well away from the lake as there was supposed to be a go, no-go signal to come from someone at the dry lake bed. From four or five miles away, the only thing we could see was a sheep camp and a band of sheep. At the appointed time, the enforcement agent made his radio call with the code and password. Someone on the ground came on with his password. They talked a little and then the radio went silent. Evidently, there had been a tip-off or something was missing in the agent's responses. We orbited the area until we were low on fuel and

Lion dogs on the Nevada ranch. "Heck" is the pup in front.

then gave up and headed for some fuel and then home.

I had hunted elk a few times and Joy's dad Lloyd, his cousin Bud Zilkey, and one of Lloyd's deer hunters from California, George Dietl, wanted to go elk hunting. We hauled a truckload of horses up from Nevada to the end of the road below Shoup, Idaho. The next morning, we got a late start down the river and towards evening we were still quite a ways from Lance's Bar where we were going to head up to hunt.

There was an old, abandoned cabin with a porch and stove and good horse feed, so we decided to camp there. George and Bud put their sleeping bags out under the porch, and Lloyd and I bedded down on the board floor in the cabin. There were cracks about an inch or so wide in the floor, and I figured the owner just swept and the debris fell through the cracks – not a bad idea! Anyway, along in the middle of the night, I sort of rolled over in my sleeping bag and was awakened by the ominous BZZZ of a rattlesnake. He had crawled up through one of the cracks and evidently decided to absorb a little warmth from my body. When I rolled over on him, he became somewhat disturbed. Hence the BUZZZ! I grabbed my flashlight and woke Lloyd with the words, "There's a snake under my sleeping bag!" Bad mistake! Lloyd jumped up, grabbed his pistol from under his pillow and went to bounding around the cabin waving the pistol. Fortunately, the snake, being blessed with a preservationist attitude, had crawled back down through the crack, and further chaos was averted. I moved my bag over the crack he had gone down, got Lloyd somewhat pacified, and we went back to sort of a fitful sleep.

We went up and camped by the Eakin Cabin and hunted out for three or four days. Lloyd went down toward Bargamin Creek one day and that night came back with a tale about a Grizzly bear scratch. He said it and the tracks were "plumb fresh." When the story was first told, Lloyd could barely reach the scratch standing on his tiptoes. As the years passed, the story was told and retold until – on tiptoes and holding his rifle at the stock – the barrel would barely reach the scratch.

Oh, yeah, we got a bull and three cows. Packed them down Dwyer Creek and up to Lance's. I'd made arrangements with Don Smith to check the sandbar at the mouth of Squaw Creek to haul meat out on his new jet boat. I took Frank Lantz over a loin of elk meat, and he invited me for supper. Lying by the porch was about a yearling black bear with a hole about four inches across through the shoulders. Frank said the bears were really tearing up his apple trees and he'd planned on scaring this one out of the tree at the corner of the porch with the .410 and bird shot. I guess he was a tad too close. After supper, topped off with sour dough biscuits from a start of sourdough that Frank had packed from West Virginia on his back, I headed back over to my sleeping bag by the four elk laid out on driftwood to cool and wait for Don the next morning. It was nearly dark and I heard a "woof" and saw the outline of a bear running away. Then it stopped and stood on its hind feet. I could barely make it out through my two power Lyman Alaskan scope but shot and killed my first bear.

Another rattlesnake story. I was flood irrigating a small alfalfa patch at our ranch in Nevada. I had put the canvas down in the ditch and was cleaning out the cut. The water came gushing out about six inches deep through the foot high alfalfa. I changed positions with my feet and about then a *big* snake tail and rattle went to beating me on the right leg. I'd evidently flooded him out and then stepped on his head. Well, I went ahead and killed him and decided to pack him to the house to show everyone because he was bigger than the ordinary snake around there. I had him over the shovel handle and over my shoulder and was about half way to the house when I stepped on a locust. He buzzed, and I threw the snake and shovel about twenty feet while I was coming

Con Hourihan with one of our mule teams that he trained.

down. Finally, I got to the house and measured the snake. He was thirty-seven inches long. Pretty big for that part of the world.

While the girls were helping me hay, I'd occasionally see a piece of equipment parked and flashes of sunlight headed toward the ground. It would be all the wrenches out of my toolbox after they ran out of rocks trying to get a snake.

In 1964, my dad was running the horses for the Boy Scout Camp out of Stanley, Idaho. One of his wranglers had lost a hunting business in Chamberlain Basin and told Dad it was for sale again. He called and asked me if I wanted to go partners on buying an elk camp if it looked like an okay deal. I said yes and would go and look at it.

The Coyote and the Fleas

One day while changing the side-roll sprinklers, I was walking through the waist-high wheat. I walked up on a half-grown coyote that started to run, but in the high grain he was not going very fast. Once again, acting on impulse, I ran after him and jumped on him. It was only about a half mile to the house so I decided to take him up to show the girls.

I got part way when I started feeling something like mosquitos on my face and neck. I slapped one and it was a big flea! Very shortly, thereafter, I didn't have enough hands to pack the coyote and swat fleas so I released the coyote.

By then, the fleas were inside my clothes and driving me crazy. I ran toward the house shedding clothes as I ran. I was nearly down to zero clothes and then down to no clothes when I raced into the house and into the shower.

Joy and the girls had gone somewhere earlier and as they drove back, they saw the trail of discarded clothing with no idea of what in world had happened. I came out of the shower and told them the whole story and we all had a good laugh.

For the next couple weeks, the coyote would sit in that field and howl. Joy said he was asking me to come back and get the rest of the fleas!

Indian Blinds in Nevada

While outfitting in Nevada, I was lucky enough to be able to spend a lot of time on top of the East Humboldt and Ruby Mountains in Elko County, Nevada. Sometimes from the top of a peak, you would look down several hundred feet to a pass or saddle across the mountain range. There, you would sometimes be able to make out some rocks that appeared to have been placed in some sort of rectangular form – seldom the same shape, but quite obviously not the work of nature.

When hiking down to the same spot, it was very hard to identify when you were actually on the spot seen from a distance. The form wasn't as obvious when you were standing right by it. I did finally find one in a pretty narrow pass, and I was able to figure out how the formation was used.

Our old Indian friends, Ed Tybo, and Chief Frank Temoke, one of my occasional team roping partners, said there were lots of bighorn sheep in that area prior to 1915. The Indians built traps to catch and kill the sheep for the meat, hides, bones, etc. Here is a sketch with approximate dimensions of one of the best ones I found up above Gray's Lake in the East Humboldt Range.

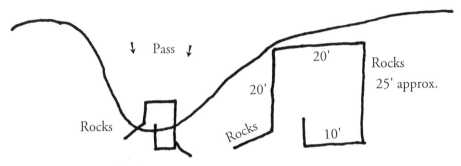

It was probably only 6 inches to a foot of rocks now, but I feel that through the years the wind had covered over with sand, dirt, and debris a corral-like structure. Most likely, if you dug down the "corral" would have been high enough to contain the sheep once they were inside.

I am assuming they had logs, poles, and/or people for wings to direct the sheep into the entrance. Then, they would block the "corral" off and probably spear or use a bow and arrow to kill the sheep.

The sheep have been transplanted back into these mountains through funding and cooperation of the Foundation for North American Wild Sheep/Nevada Bighorns Unlimited and the Nevada Division of Wildlife. There are limited tags available to hunt them at this time.

The Indians also trapped sage hens out in the flats by weaving blankets of sagebrush bark. With the "blankets" help up by brush, they would drive the birds toward and under the fibrous nets, trapping them as they tried to fly away.

This historic Indian blind in the Lost River Range in Idaho is near where Stan killed his big ram. Sheep trails go on both sides of the blind.

Chapter 10

My Law Enforcement Career

During one of the lean times (which was most of the time) on the ranch in Nevada, I was in Quilici's Market buying groceries. The Wells Chief of Police, Bunny Powers, asked me if I would be interested in being the relief patrolman.

He had three full-time officers and said if I could work about ten days a month he could schedule their time off to fit my days.

We needed any extra money we could make, so I was surely interested but told him I had no experience. He said it was no problem, as all there was to do was check locks after the businesses closed up and drink coffee. His son-in-law, Earl Supp, would break me in.

I showed up the first afternoon, was issued a badge, gun, handcuffs, tear gas, etc., and took the oath.

We were driving around town a few minutes later when we received a radio call that there was a disturbance at The Hacienda, one of the local cathouses.

We drove across the tracks, and the madam met us at the door. A gunman had one of the girls in a room threatening to kill her.

We talked our way in and got his gun and handcuffed him. On the floor was one of those old-fashioned lunch buckets that holds a Thermos® bottle in the lid. We opened it up, and it was FULL OF MONEY!

He said he'd been herding sheep for his uncle up in Idaho and Unc had paid him off in cash.

We took him to jail, and about then we got a call from the Twin Falls Police. The guy had robbed a bank in Idaho Falls, held up a taxi driver and forced him to drive to Wells.

Here I was two hours into my law enforcement career of checking locks and drinking coffee and had captured a bank robber with a gun at the local House of Ill Repute!

It's seldom simple when Potts does it.

No bull, the elk in this picture was a "royal cow elk" taken by Chuck Rouland in October of 1972. The antlers of this cow elk scored out at 358 Boone and Crockett points.

Chapter 11

How We Got Started in Outfitting

Joy and I got married in 1954 and we were living in her uncle's house in Mackay. That fall after the ranch work was mostly done, I was working for the local John Deere dealer, Andy Hintze, putting equipment together. The plows, discs, balers, etc., came in on the train and had to be unloaded and put together for display and sale. One Friday evening a vacuum cleaner salesman came by trying to sell us a vacuum. God knows we needed one as we had not much of anything, including and especially money! Our house was furnished in what Joy called "Early Matrimonial," whatever we could borrow or someone would give us.

The salesman was from Blackfoot and was going deer hunting. The wheels slowly started to turn and I proposed a trade. I would take some horses, camp gear, food, etc., up into the deer country and trade him a weekend deer hunting for the vacuum cleaner. Well, we got the trade together – I borrowed dad's truck and some horses and gear and away we went to the North Fork of the Big Lost River. This was about twenty-five miles from town and I knew it to be good deer country.

We hunted part of the day and set up camp. (What one of my later hunters would call the "no frill's camp.") Frying pan, coffee pot, plates, cups, etc., and a couple of sleeping bags under the truck bed. And here was WHERE I should have taken heed and remembered a little better when I decided to become a real outfitter.

The next morning I built a fire, made some coffee, started breakfast, and called my hunter. After a few minutes he hollered for some help. I went around the truck and here was the scenario. He had somehow zipped himself into the sleeping bag with his hands inside where he couldn't reach the zipper to unzip! Don't ask me how. No idea. BUT, a prelude to some of the pitfalls and tribulations of, at present, forty-three years as an outfitter.

Summer pack trip with nine people from Vancouver, British Columbia.

Outfitting in Idaho

I called the guy that had the outfitting business for sale and made arrangements to look at it. His name was Louis Bicandi, and he lived in Homedale, Idaho. I told him I would fly up to McCall, Idaho, meet him there and we would fly into Chamberlain. He had a lease on a Fish & Game ranch in there called the Hotzel Ranch with an old dirt floor cabin, a horse corral, and a fenced meadow where the horses were kept. I was in the flying club still and we'd traded the Aeronca Champ for a 90 hp Super Cub. I'd not done any mountain flying but knew that Chamberlain had good approaches and was plenty long even for a novice pilot. I met him in McCall, and we flew over to Chamberlain. Flying over those mountains, the first thing I noticed was the small percentage of places you could land versus the large percentage of nothing but trees and rocks.

The outfit looked pretty good. He had eighteen head of stock, fair gear, and tents and quite a few hunters booked. He was in the middle of a divorce and really wanted out. He wanted $5,000 for the outfit. I told him if he would stay and help me find and get the camps set up, we would give him $1,000 down and pay him off in four years. One of the problems was the pricing structure of the hunts. We inherited about twenty hunters and the spike camp hunts were booked at $100 per person with one-on-one guided hunts at $350 for ten days!

We got the deal put together about the first of August and the season opened mid September. I told him to come in on Sept. 1 to help me get the four camps set up.

He came in and we set up the closest camp at Little Lodgepole Creek, an early camp, close to the trail and only about one hour from the ranch. The next day he said he had to call a plane and fly out. Something about his divorce and he'd be back the following day. That was the last time I ever laid eyes on Louis Bicandi.

Dad was still with the Boy Scouts so I was kind of alone until three or four days before elk season. I was able to get some gear together and find the camps at Hot Spring Meadow, Queens Creek and Quaking Aspen Spring and get some rough camps set up. However, I didn't have any time to scout or learn the country.

I had called some of my deer hunters from the Nevada camp and was able to get a few of them to come to Chamberlain for elk and deer. I would take the hunters to camp, get them fed and put to bed and then ride out in the dark a few miles to at least learn which way to leave camp in the morning. Not the best way to run a railroad, but the best I could do under the circumstances.

The next year we had some time to learn the country, pour a floor of concrete in the old Hotzel cabin and cut logs for another cabin. One of Dad's old friends Jess Taylor from Big Creek wrote Dad and asked if we would be interested in helping him with his hunters or leasing his hunting business. I was sure interested, as Jess was one of the old time bighorn sheep guides and I wanted to learn something about sheep and goat hunting. We didn't have sheep hunting in Chamberlain. So, we leased the Taylor Ranch area the next year. The plan was to do most of the elk hunting at Chamberlain until late October and then move the stock to the Taylor Ranch to hunt elk and deer until the end of the season which was in early December back then. We would take a small string to the Taylor Ranch early for sheep hunting and some elk hunting.

Dad went to the Taylor Ranch the next year, and Joy and I ran Chamberlain. Dad and Mr. Taylor didn't get along very well so we switched, and Joy and I went to the Taylor Ranch the following year. We had bought a Cessna 180 so it was a lot easier to get back and forth if we were needed at the other place. This worked out real well and I was getting a chance to hunt some sheep. There was no draw then – open season – so it was just a matter of booking the hunters. In 1968, there were thirty-six rams taken in Idaho and nine of them came from my camp. Plus, we were getting $750 per man for sheep hunts. There would never be another poor day!

Some years, the high passes between Chamberlain and Big Creek would have a lot of snow. One year the storms came early and Joy and I left Chamberlain with the horses before daylight. It was fifty miles to the Taylor Ranch and we were going to try to make it in one day. I was leading a small string and Joy was following the rest of them loose. These horses hadn't seen any grass that didn't have snow on it for a month or so. When we got over the top and were coming down Coxie Creek and got below the snow line, the loose horses scattered out onto those grassy ridges and really gave Joy fits. Also, it slowed our travel to a crawl. We had about ten miles to go, and it was starting to get dark, plus Joy was bushed from riding up and down the hills trying to keep the horses moving. We found a place we could turn all the stock loose and bed down ahead of them. We had a little food and our sleeping bags. It was getting pretty cold. I had been packing one of those metal matches and had never had to use it. I built us a nice fire with my metal match.

When the season ended, we then would take the horses out to Challis and truck them back to the ranch in Nevada for the winter. The

The biggest load I ever had to put on a mule! It weighed 400 pounds. Look at Tillie's face.

other outfitters in the area, Cold Meadows and the Root Ranch, would usually come through and stay with us at the Taylor Ranch. Some years we would take all the stock out together and overnight the next night at the Flying B. One year the Root Ranch and Cal Stoddard came through and stayed with us. We all headed out the next morning. I was in the lead with a small string and there were 110 total head of stock, about one-half mile long single file. About two miles down the trail just past Goat Creek, the trail was washed out about twenty feet wide on a near vertical slope. The ground was frozen and there was about one inch of fresh snow. I got off, got my axe off my horse and walked up to see if I could cross to cut a tree to start a repair job. I slipped and fell down the chute probably fifty feet, bouncing on the rocks and trying to hold the axe where I wouldn't fall on it. I lucked out with no major wounds. I was able to pull myself back up about the time the first guys got around the horses to see what was wrong.

 We cut one long tree and tied it along the downhill side where the outside of the trail had been, then many four foot poles to angle into the bank. Then many rocks on them and all the dirt we could chip loose on top. Pretty shaky but it worked!

 We had lost probably three hours here and the days are short in December. I headed on down Big Creek toward the Middle Fork of the

Heading to Stoddard Lake from Cold Meadows airstrip with a family that is going fishing in the Frank Church Wilderness.

Salmon. About one mile from the Middle Fork is a solid bridge called Bighorn Bridge. It's maybe seventy feet wide. When I got up to it, I couldn't believe my eyes. A large rock (one ton model) had rolled off the mountain and gone through the center of the bridge! Here we go again! Fall trees, limb them, cut them about ten feet long, drag them up and cover the hole. It had to be solid so a horse wouldn't step through and get hung up. Once again we were under way, but it was nearly dark and about fifteen miles to go. No options about camping until morning with 110 horses from three different strings.

There was still a lot of excitement to go. A lot of the Root Ranch horses were loose and carrying riding saddles or empty packsaddles. They knew where the Flying B was, and it was their winter range and home. They wanted to end this nonsense of plodding along the trail and started passing each other, passing the strings being led, passing above the trail, below the trail, knocking horses off the trail and generally causing havoc. The only good thing was it was dark and all you could see were the sparks from their feet and from the rocks rolling toward the river. How we kept from wasting a bunch I'll never know. The ones that got around the strings and headed on to the Flying B bypassed the bridge and just went to the mountain. Three days later they were still rounding up to retrieve saddles and pull shoes.

The Wolf Pack in Chamberlain

In 1964, the year we bought the Chamberlain Basin hunting business, I had a unique experience. My dad and I and four hunters were headed for Hot Springs Meadows to hunt elk and deer. I was in the lead just past Queen's Creek. There was about four inches of new snow and I could see a large group of tracks intersecting the trail in front of me. I expected to see that a herd of elk had crossed and rode on up to check the direction and age of the tracks with the idea of maybe making a hunt on them. When I got to the tracks, I couldn't believe my eyes. A large pack of wolves had come onto the trail and was moving ahead of me. The tracks were only an hour or so old.

We counted the tracks as best we could and figured there were about twelve wolves. The smallest tracks were about the size of a dog coyote and the largest track was about like a big tom lion. After a mile, the wolves left the trail and headed over toward the breaks of the Salmon River and the head of Bear Creek. We headed on towards Hot Springs and about one-half mile above the camp I jumped some elk. I jumped off as I didn't have my elk, and we could use some meat on the

Cold Meadows Guard Station. I led nineteen head about fifteen miles with only one broken pigtail!

hunt. I shot a calf with my .30/.30, dressed it right quick as it was getting dark. We threw it over my saddle, tied it down, and went on to camp.

Now the blood was dripping into the snow down the hill across the meadow and to the tree by the tents where we hung the elk. Dad and I unpacked and I unsaddled while he lit lanterns, unmantied and started supper. We fed the hunters and everyone headed for bed while I was finishing the dishes. Over the noise of the clanking of the dishes, I heard what I thought was a bull bugle. About then Dad said, "Come listen to this." I went out and the wolf pack was coming down the hill on our tracks with the fresh blood trail. They were howling like banshees. Talk about the hair standing up on the back of your neck! We had the bell on Boise, Dad's gelding. I jumped back to the tent, got my gun and a flashlight and as I came back, the horses and mules were coming out of the meadow and lining up head to tail in the light that reflected from the lantern in the three tents. All of them but Boise and I could hear his bell out in the direction of the wolf howls. I ran out into the meadow shining the light and hollering. The howls quit as soon as they had started. I found Boise and brought him back closer but the wolves did not come back.

The next day, one of the hunters ran into them and shot one of the pups. He was about the size of a small coyote. Impossible! Right.

There were no native wolves back there. That's why they brought the transplants to us from Canada. My dad and all the hunters were dead when they interviewed me about it so I had no one to verify the story. The printed word that was put out was that "There is a rumor by an outfitter" of wolves in central Idaho. That winter at the outfitters meeting, I talked to Ken Wolfinhager about it. He said sure, we have wolves around most winters. His idea was that they had crossed on the ice and were really some of the wolves from the Selway. They were sighted around there for several years including on the airstrip by the ranger from the Chamberlain Guard Station.

Selling Chamberlain and Buying Taylor Ranch Business

After a few years of running both the Chamberlain Basin and Taylor Ranch hunting businesses under a lease, we felt that maybe we were spread too thin. I was trying to do as much of the flying as I could to help the bottom line plus guiding and packing during the hunts. I'd come out with a group of hunters and load them, gear, meat, horns, etc., and head for Boise. I'd unload there, load a new group and head to one of the camps. Sometimes the weather would not be flyable and problems would stack up. Plus, my dad was getting older and wanted to slow down if he could. So, we sold the Chamberlain Basin Outfitters business

Tom Scheth with "first bull"!

to Scott and Shelda Farr, Dad went into semi-retirement, and Joy and I bought the Taylor Ranch hunting business from Jess and Dorothy Taylor. We would have liked to buy the ranch itself but were just a little late. The University of Idaho had obtained an option on it and ultimately exercised that option. We leased part of the ranch facilities from the University. In 1977, we sold the Taylor Ranch business to one of our guides, Con Hourihan, and slowed down a little. We took a few sheep hunters only for a few years and then purchased the business we still have that is just north of the Taylor Ranch area, but we are able to access it mostly by pack string and don't have to use aircraft nearly so much.

Walking Rush Creek

When we were at the Taylor Ranch, Jess and Dorothy Taylor were still there so we got to do a lot of visiting about Cougar Dave Lewis and his early years on Big Creek. Jess told me that Cougar Dave was the only guy that had walked Rush Creek, so I kept it in the back of my mind.

One year we were coming out from Telephone Creek with

Stan Potts on Henry. Never turn stock loose with their halters on. Henry hooked his on a log and choked to death.

Stan Potts and Stan Christiansen with an 8x8 bull elk. Note the double droppers on each side.

hunters, making good time, plenty of help, so I decided I would hike the creek while the string went up the Dead-Horse Trail and around by Rush Point Lookout to the Ranch. I took my lunch and my .30/.30 and headed down the creek. About a half mile into my walk, I came upon the fresh horn of a bighorn ram lying on a sandbar in the creek. I knew the carcass or other horn would be somewhere near. It was really brushy, but after a couple of hours, I found the carcass with the other horn in a cave where a bear had dragged it. I didn't have a pack frame so just tied the skull over my back with my jacket wrapped around it to sort of cushion my head and shoulders. This had set me back, and I still had probably six or seven air miles to go and it was probably 4:00 p.m. by now.

    I hurried as fast as I could but the bear trails through the brush along the creek would vanish. I would go to the creek and walk into the water as it was usually only about a foot deep. The rocks were slick so that was slow going. When I'd come to deep water, I'd do the best I could, sometimes having to go up around cliffs and rocks. Fish would swim ahead of me and then go to the side just like they wanted to get a first hand look at this strange creature that had invaded their domain. Same with a water ouzel. He'd fly down stream, find a rock to perch on, and wait for me to catch up or go by. Then on ahead and do it again.

I could hear the increase in noise from the gorge below me and supposed to not be passable. I had flown it and other than a big logjam, I couldn't see anything that I thought I couldn't get around. I knew I wanted to get by it in the daylight so kept hurrying. When I got to the logjam, I decided I'd just walk the logs that paralleled the stream. The jam was probably eight or ten feet above the water and 200 or 300 yards long. Big rocks and small waterfalls under it, hence the roar from the gorge. I was nearly across the jam when I slipped and fell backwards. The sheep horns and skull cracked into my skull, and I was nearly knocked out but able to catch myself and get on through. I figured if I could make the Lewis Fork of Rush Creek by dark, I might be able to walk the rest of the way in the dark and by moon light as it was a lot flatter water and wider in the bottom. Just before dark, I noticed a smoke blackened ledge on my right. I maneuvered over close to it and spotted a big cave up about twenty feet above it, also smoke blackened, but several of the rocks had slabbed off so I couldn't get up to it. The charcoal on top of the sand was interspersed with cracked bone chips. Definitely an exciting find as this was the area of the last Indian war in the United States that had ended only ninety years before. I made a note to return and check it out the next available time.

I knew the moon would come up after dark and went as far as I could. When I couldn't see, I pulled out and lay down to rest. Probably got an hour of rest and fitful sleep when the moonlight started down the western ridges. Rush Creek flows north and the moon never made it to the bottom of its canyon. The hills to the east were just too high. However, the reflection from 100 yards or so up the hill gave me enough light to get on in. It was about 10:00 when I walked into the cookhouse. Joy and Tom Palmier, one of our hunters that was wheelchair bound, were the only ones still up. They fed me and listened to my tale.

The next day I went up to show my sheep horns to Jess. He was impressed with the sheep horns but not by my feat of walking Rush Creek. His words, "Dave walked it in the winter on the ice!" He didn't add it, but I could almost hear the rest, "You dummy!"

A few years later, we had sold the Taylor Ranch business to Con Hourihan. Joy and I and our son-in-law, Jerry Black, were going to help him on a hunt. We flew in a couple of days early, and I asked Joy and Jerry if they wanted to hike up Rush Creek to the cave, spend the night and explore it and come out the next day. The answer was, "You bet!"

The Idaho wilderness, setting of our outfitting business.

I figured we could make it an easy one-half day, but we barely made it by dark. The next morning we got a small log about twenty-five feet long and leaned it up against the floor of the cave. Jerry was able to climb up it. (Evidently, when the face had slabbed off after the Indians were gone, it took the hand and foot holds to access the cave with it). Jerry gave us a report; about one foot of pine needles covered the floor of the cave. As he kicked around to the floor, he kicked out lots of bones and threw them down to us. We laid them all on a flat rock. It was weird. The bones consisted of the lower jawbones and scapulas from the mountain sheep. This may have been a small family of Indians that avoided the soldiers. I'd like to think so.

The Bobcat/The Sheep/The Elk

When you spend a lot of time in the mountains, you sometimes get to see and experience things that are almost impossible to fathom. One such instance transpired like this. Joy had drawn a sheep tag and she and I had been hunting for about a week trying to find a good ram for her. We had a pretty good camp set up and were splitting up so we could glass more country and from different drainages. As I neared the

Remnants of bighorn sheep found in a Sheepeaters' cave in the Idaho wilderness.

top of the mountain, I spotted a fairly large herd of mountain sheep coming around the mountain towards me. I sat down and was looking through the trees trying to spot a good ram. I knew the chances were slim as they were mostly ewes and lambs. While looking through the trees, I noticed a large bobcat behind a tree from the sheep but on my side of the tree. He was in a crouch and I could tell he was planning on mountain mutton for supper. The sheep were tightly bunched and walking and trotting daintily toward me in a line that would put them right by the bobcat's tree. As the sheep were just about to the tree, maybe ten feet away, I could see the cat tense to jump on one. At that exact moment, directly behind me and only a few feet away, came an ungodly blood-curdling scream! In my mind's eye, I could see three things happening at once. I jerked my head around to see a cow elk that nearly stepped on me feeding into me crosswind and I hidden by a log and small tree. She had let out the scream! (I must have really smelled bad)! Quickly looking back, I saw that the sheep herd had stampeded toward the bobcat, and he was being run over and trampled by a herd of sheep! It was like a movie in slow motion. Bobcat would take a flip down the hill and more sheep would run over him in their panic. I bet he flipped four or five times before things unraveled and he got

Stan Potts and packstring.

untangled from the sheep herd. He sort of slunk off behind them wondering about what had spoiled his perfect setup. No, there were no big rams in the bunch, but after twenty-one days, Joy made a one-shot kill on a beautiful ram that scored 164 Boone & Crockett points.

Horse Mountain Sheep Horns

In 1968, we had a group of sheep hunters including Dan Galbraith, the owner of the Pittsburgh Pirates, his doctor, and his attorney. It was September and the World Series was on with Pittsburgh in the Series. Mr. Galbraith and his vice president Bob Edler had both gotten nice rams. We took them back to the Taylor Ranch where I could care for the hides and fly the meat out to a cooler. The rest of the group including my good friends and guides Dick Hall and Fay Detweiler were still looking for more rams.

Mr. Galbraith and I were out in the middle of Big Creek fly-fishing and listening to the World Series on his belt radio when one of his players, Mattie Alou, dropped a fly ball and the other team won a game. Dan rolled in his fly line and said, "I guess you better fly me out so I can go back and keep track of what's happening."

The next day I decided to take some fresh food and go see if I

Horse Mountain sheep horns.

Cradle Camp before the big fire (pre-1988).

A "beautiful" forest after the 1988 fire.

could help the hunters that were still hunting. As I brought my little packstring up the mountains, one of the sub-guides met me on the trail. He said they had gotten a ram the day before and shot at another one. He showed me where to go meet up with the guys. When I got there, they showed me where they had shot at the other ram. I told them to wait where they were and direct me to the exact spot where the ram had been standing when the shot was fired. I wanted to see if I could find where the bullet had hit, plus look for blood and hair.

They got me to the spot and I was unable to find anything but started following the tracks. In a short distance, one of the rams had left the rest and took off straight downhill in big bounding jumps. Now, this is a strong indication of a possible solid hit. I followed the track a couple hundred yards and sat down to glass ahead. I saw a magpie in a bush and put the binoculars on him. Underneath I could see a ram horn. I thought, "Damn, we have wasted a ram." I went down, and to my surprise, the running ram track went right on by the horn. The ram horn that I had spotted was actually two old weathered ram heads lying side by side. I followed the ram track for a few hundred yards, but there was still no sign of a hit. I went back and tied the two ram skulls on my

Jim Solecki and guide Mitch McFarland with the best bighorn we have ever taken, a 187-point ram.

pack frame and headed back up to the guys. Naturally, when they saw ram horns, they thought I had found their ram.

These horns had lain on that mountain for very many years. There were no other bones around so it was nearly certain that they had been killed by someone for meat. The only person living back there thirty to seventy years before was Cougar Dave Lewis. I feel very strongly that he had killed these two rams for meat, and I left the heads because they were of no practical use. The heads were both a very unique shape that we call the Argalli style. Nearly identical in shape but one quite a bit larger. I'm certain the rams were very closely related. The larger ram had exactly forty inch horns on both sides and a twelve inch third quarter, and allowing for some horn at the base that was rotted out, he scored about 186 Boone & Crockett points. A great and beautiful head that we still have on our wall.

The "misery whip" with Pat Hendren, left, and Jack Basolo at the right, with Larry Stark working as supervisor. Stan Potts, photographer. Eh! Eh!

The series of six photographs on this and the following two pages shows an especially bad time in my outfitting years. In this case, bad times came in the form of forest fires. In 1988 I lost all my camps to fire, which devastated the camps, as the photographs so clearly demonstrate. I had to give my clients their money back and nearly went broke.

Bad times are made up by the good times! Granddaughter Addie Maxfield (top photo) and grandson Tim Maxfield (bottom) at Stoddard Lake with "The Old Guy".

Chapter 12

Airplanes and Unscheduled Landings

2242 Charlie

Through the years we have been lucky enough to own several airplanes (usually *we* and some bank!). We bought a 1953 Cessna 180-2242 Charlie in late 1969 and flew it about 700 hours until March of 1974, when a windstorm jerked our tie-downs out and it landed upside down on the old highway at the ranch.

We bid $1,500 on the salvage but lost the bid by $50 to a salvage buyer from Oklahoma. (So far, it was the best airplane we ever owned!) One year we flew it from the tip of Baja California to above the Arctic Circle!

I had one unscheduled landing at the Taylor Ranch with "Charlie" when I lost all my oil from a faulty oil filter cap.

"Charlie" sitting 90 miles south of the Arctic Circle.

Charlie after the windstorm.

"Mixmaster"

We then bought a 1964 Cessna 336-N4633 and flew it about seventy hours. It was a great performer, but the maintenance and repairs were eating us up. I had a cowl flap motor burn out taking off from Twin Falls with a heavy load of grain and ruined the rear engine from overheating.

We were members of the Baja Bush Pilots, a group of fliers that flew to Baja several times a year. One year we took the 336. (We called it the "Mixmaster" and "Bucket of Bumblebees.") We played some of their flying games and were awarded their "2Holer" award. They would load your plane to gross weight and you had to make five consecutive takeoffs and landings inside a distance 10 percent over your minimum takeoff and landing distance. It penciled out about 660' in the sand, and we did it. The other pilots couldn't believe how it performed.

We were on a whale watching expedition, and because the Skymaster was the noisiest plane, I got to be the one who would try to make the whales breech so a camera plane behind me could film them.

I made one pass probably twenty feet off the water, and the whale didn't come up. Arnold Senterfitt radioed me that I was too high!

On the way back from Baja and south of Ely, Nev., the oil pressure on the rear engine started to rise very high. I'd never had that happen, so I throttled back and radioed Ely. Ferrel Gale, the owner and mechanic, told me to stop in and run the engine as lightly as I dared. We had lots of altitude and weren't heavily loaded so it was no problem. He found that the probe wire had broken and was grounding against the engine. He fixed it, and we were on our way.

The next day I took it to Twin Falls for an oil change, and about fifteen miles south of Twin Falls the oil pressure on that same engine started to go down. When I was to the red line, I shut that engine off and flew on in using the front engine – the least efficient of the two engines. When I turned off the runway, I looked back and a trail of oil was following me. My old friend and mechanic Pete Lazaros found a broken oil line, and it pumped all the oil out. I was lucky and didn't hurt the engine.

The times we were in Baja with that plane was about the only times something wasn't going wrong with it.

I kept calling the guys I bought it from, and they said to bring it back and they would fix it. We were going to the sports show in San Francisco for about ten days, so I asked if they could have it ready during that time. You bet, no problem!

We came back over to Hayward to leave for home, and there was the airplane scattered all over the hangar floor!

"No problem!" The owner said, "Take my Aztec."

"But you don't understand – I don't have a multi-engine rating."

Downstream take-off at the Taylor Ranch.

"No problem! I'll show you how to fly it."

So, nearing darkness, we went around the patch about three times at Hayward. He cut one engine on me once. We lit and taxied back. I wasn't sure I could even start it!

I loaded Joy, and we headed out over the Sierras into the darkness. Joy's words while we were climbing out: "Potts, we have done some stupid things in our lives, but this may be the worst."

Yeah, about then the windows started to ice over. Joy had the book open trying to figure out how to start the heaters/defrosters. It was a kerosene set-up and you push Button A, flip Toggle Switch B and it starts. After three or four false tries it started, so we headed on to Wells in the darkness and made an uneventful night landing. How? I'm not sure.

The next morning I called Mike Loening in Boise and told him I needed someone to teach me how to fly an Aztec. He said, "I don't even want to know how you got it to Wells, but bring it up and I'll get you taught and rated." I got my multi-engine rating on Jan. 29, 1975 in 4904P.

The 336 was ready, so I flew back, returned their Aztec and headed for Wells – once again in the darkness. Somewhere west of Battle Mountain, Nev., I noticed my lights were dimming. My radios were getting weak and VOR needles wouldn't budge. A total electrical failure! I turned east because I knew Battle Mountain was somewhere in that direction. I found the town

Our 206, the load hauler.

and the airstrip but no lighted windsock, so I couldn't tell which way the wind was blowing. I've got my flashlight in my teeth aimed primarily at the airspeed. I can't get any flaps down but finally decide on my direction of landing. Luckily, I had learned to land without landing lights so not having them was okay. Luckily there was no wind.

I got it stopped and then tried to find a way off the runway. No lighted taxiways! I was taxing up and down the strip with my flashlight out the window trying to find a way to get to the hangars, when I saw car lights coming toward me. When he got there, I got out and told him my problem. He said, "I could hear this plane flying around but no lights, so I came to see if I could help." I followed him to the gas pumps, shut off the plane, and tied it down. He gave me a ride to town, and I called Joy and told here of my exciting ride – then I had about six martinis to calm my jangled nerves.

I decided it was never going to work right, so I put it up for sale. I got a call to bring it to Elko, and the guy would come in on the United flight to look at it. It was Friday afternoon and two guys showed up. We flew around, and they made me an offer way less than I wanted. I came down a little, and we finally reached a price.

They opened up their briefcase, and there were bundles of freshly minted $100 bills. I figured they'd made them the night before.

Joy and Stan Potts at the Taylor Ranch, and our bulls in 1980. The big pickup head scored 187 and was stolen from us.

I looked at my watch, and it was about 5:15 p.m. I called a banker friend of mine, Ron Wetzel, and he was still at the bank. I told him my problem, and he said he'd wait and check out the money. The bills were okay.

I asked the guys what they were going to do about insurance. Their words: "Where this plane is going, we don't need insurance."

Cessna 206P & Cessna 180

We then bought a 1968 Cessna 206P model 8647Z (Zulu) from Dirk Agee, a rancher friend at O'Neil, Nev., and flew it about 450 hours through 1979. It was a great plane and a real load hauler. It had a full Robertson Kit and turbo-charged engine.

We had sold the Taylor Ranch hunting business, so we didn't need to haul heavy loads. I sold it to a friend, Jay Sevy, and bought a 1973 Cessna 180-9715G from another friend in Sun Valley, Bob Stevens. He had purchased it new when he was flying for Frontier Airlines. It was a good plane with no problems. We flew it about 150 hours over the next few years and sold it to Howard Hash in Stevensville, Montana.

M4 Maule

I borrowed and rented airplanes until May of 1998, when we bought an M4 Maule-2058U. I flew it about 60 hours and then had the misfortune of breaking it through some hard snow at our airstrip at Colson Creek. It tipped on its nose. Didn't have any insurance so had to sell it to pay for the new prop and repairs (but salvaged enough money to buy a backhoe and old dump truck that we really needed).

Kitfox Model 5

I'd been building on a Kitfox Model 5 for the past five years, so I got pretty serious to get it flying. We started it in the basement of the house and actually had the wings on it from corner to corner with about six inches to spare on each end.

This was my first experience at building an aircraft, and because we are so far from the mainstream I wasn't able to get much help. We joined the Experimental Aircraft Association, but the closest chapter is in Idaho Falls. No one was able to come help or even take a look at it. A few calls to the factory for assistance was the best I could do.

I trailered it over to Challis for the final assembly and some technical help from Pete Nelson at Middle Fork Aviation. I'd also made arrangements with the FAA for my inspection and initial test flight out of there.

Our Maule before and after I tipped it on its nose.

The first flight was about five minutes long. Up and down. Controls, etc., worked as normal, but I had a valve stick in the engine. It's a high time 100 h.p. Continental and hadn't run for several years. Pete helped me pull the valve. There was a rough burr on the valve stem.

I buffed it smooth and we put it back together. In the next nine hours of test flying there were no problems – except making it land and stay down. It wanted to come back into the air. Practicing crosswind landings at May, Idaho, I dropped it in too hard and collapsed the right gear leg with prop strike, bent prop and wingtip damage. I'm now fixing it up to try and get it rigged right for landing.

I had quite a few spectators, mostly pilots, watching my first test flight. Several had from 5,000 to 20,000 hours. When I came back and they congratulated me, they told me that not one of them had ever made the maiden voyage in an aircraft. Right then, I felt like a real test pilot, but not when I bent it up.

Up the Yukon River.

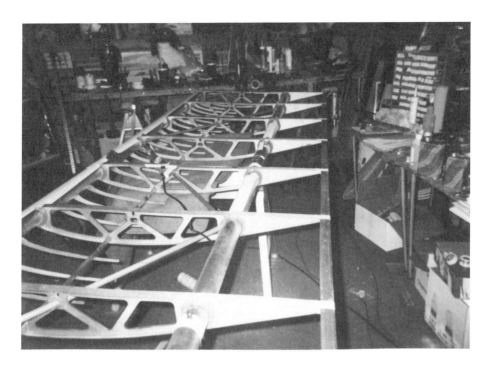

Building plane in basement.

For fuel flow test in climb attitude.

Damn!

Commercial License and Instrument Rating

I had managed to get a commercial license in 1971. In 1976, a good friend of ours, Ken Johnson, was very ill with Leukemia. Joy and I went down to Los Altos, Calif., and stayed with him for a month or so. During that time, I kept my plane at Reed Hillview Airport and took instruction for my instrument rating. I passed my checkride on the second try on Feb. 20, 1976.

My bighorn ram and three more in 1968.

Chapter 13

My Grand Slam

Since I was a young man, I had been an avid reader of *Outdoor Life, Argosy, Field & Stream*, and other outdoor books. Some of them had stories by Jack O'Connor and others about sheep hunting and the collection of the four different species of sheep in North America. It was a distant, vague dream and wish that I would be able to someday hunt them all.

When I started outfitting for bighorn sheep in Idaho, there was a general season so you just bought a tag. I'd buy one every year thinking if the situation was right, I'd get me a ram and I was able to get a nice ram in 1968. It seemed there were rams all over that year. We figured I had seen a total of twenty-five different legal rams that fall and mine was the ninth one we collected.

We were living in Nevada, which had quite a few desert bighorn sheep. (They now have Rocky Mountain Bighorns and California Bighorns through the transplant program). The tags were by drawing and some of my friends had drawn and killed rams. In fact, when the seasons were first opened, it was not a very popular sport and some guys had drawn two or three years in a row. It had become more popular by the time I started putting in. Joy and I and Kay would put in each year. Kay drew first and we didn't get her a ram. Found some, spent all day getting there to find the spot where someone had killed one and the rest disappeared. We found out later it was a lady hunter that had gotten her ram. We would put in for the bombing range out of Las Vegas and east of Yucca Flats where they were testing the atom bombs. This hunt was for two weeks through Christmas and New Year's each year.

The next tag drawn was Joy's, and we found rams all over. We figured we saw forty-seven rams in two weeks with twenty-seven legal. She got a shot at a ram I figured could have been the world's record. It was a tough 400-yard shot in high winds. She did what I told her, and I was wrong on the hold and she shot over the ram. We then passed up a lot of good rams looking for him again. The next to last day she hit a very nice ram, and we went to the end of the season trying to get him. She got a shot and missed, and we watched the ram run out across the desert the last day of the season.

On the seventh year of my applying, I finally drew. This year the rams were scarce. In the first week, we had not found even a legal ram. We were splitting up again trying to find something to hunt. One evening when we got back to our tent in the desert, Joy said she had found two good ram tracks in the snow coming over to our side of the mountain. The next morning I went that way and about three miles up the canyon, I spotted them, two legal desert rams!

Stan Potts with first bighorn, 1968.

I sneaked up with about 125 yards trying to decide which one. One was probably thirty-five inches – thirty-six inch horns but fairly thin on the ends, barely starting to broom, or break off the horn tips so he could see past them. The other was shorter horns but broomed back to three-quarter curl or less. He had lots of character, and I decided to take him. I had my movie camera and set it up on the tripod hoping I could get it high enough over the hideout rock to get some footage. However, these sheep have eyes like eagles, and I finally decided I'd better quit trying to be Camera Man and become Sheep Hunter. Two shots and I was half way to the Grand Slam!

Dr. Hansen at the Corn Creek Field Station wanted a ram brought back whole if anyone could. I was so stoked I figured I could do it.

(Probably could have but I had my gun, spotting scope, binoculars, etc., also.). I packed everything for about one mile and decided I'd have to clean the ram. I removed the intestines and lungs and that was enough less weight that I packed him on to the Jeep okay. They really needed the liver, kidneys, heart, etc., to test for radioactivity from the atom bomb testing. (In fact, one year we couldn't go in to start the hunt because of a bomb test. The tests were made a long way underground but we could see the mushroom cloud in the sky just like Hiroshima). The ram weighted 105 pounds the way I brought him in. He was six years old and the largest horn was thirty-one inches.

Now I had the two hardest sheep so it was mostly a matter of money to get to the north country for the other two. When I sold the ranch in Nevada, I did what any sensible person would do with some of the money. I booked a white sheep hunt with Stan Reynolds in the Yukon!

Joy went along as basically a non-hunter but wanted a nice caribou if we saw one. We took our friend and guide Dick Hall along to hunt also as our guest. We would be hunting for whatever we wanted, as the laws then were that you bought a hunting license and then at the end of the hunt, you paid a trophy fee for the different animals you had taken. We took our Cessna 180 2242C, and flew to Penticton, British Columbia, and then on to Vanderhorf, B.C, where some friends from Nevada, George and Susy

My grand slam, finished with the Stone ram on the right in 1974.

Stan Potts and Desert ram taken in Nevada.

Shumann had bought a ranch. The town airstrip was on their ranch and we stayed all night with them.

We were getting ready to leave the next morning, planning to follow the Alaska Highway to White Horse. A couple of natives who were working on their plane at the airport asked us where we were headed. We told them and they said, "Why don't you fly the trench? It saves you about 300 miles." They showed us on our maps and told us the only fuel was at Ingeneka. It was too far to the next fuel at Watson Lake, Yukon, without fueling somewhere. We decided to try it, filed a flight plan to Watson Lake, Yukon, and took off. This is through what they called "Uninhabited Territories." If you were over thirty minutes overdue on a flight plan, the search would start and the *searchee* would pay for it. I decided to add an hour on my e.t.a. because of that. We were going to be flying up the Tilletson Reservoir for 150 miles and Ingeneka was part way up it. The reservoir had a huge hydro plant to serve southern and western BC and the northern U.S. They had fallen the trees inside the water line and as the water level backed up, the trees floated. They were hauling the logs to mills with big tugboats pulling one-half mile of logs yarded together. Pretty awesome to three desert rats from Nevada where a three foot wide creek was major water!

When we got to Ingeneka, they had told us to buzz a little Indian encampment and someone would bring fuel up to the airstrip about a mile away. We did and pretty soon a white man named Sims brought a fifty-gallon barrel of gas on the bucket of a little Ford tractor. He was the outfitter in the area and married to one of the Indian ladies. We fueled up and went on to Watson Lake and fueled again redoing our flight plan to Whitehorse, Yukon. The weather was getting worse the further we went, and we finally had to put down at Teslin Lake. It rained for about two days straight and our cushion of time was running out. Finally, I heard a plane go over from the north. I got on the radio and he had made it through from Whitehorse. He said that after we got on past the end of Teslin Lake the weather got better onto Whitehorse and beyond. He said to hug the shoreline on the west side of the lake until we got through it.

We filed for Whitehorse, took off and made it without incident. We fueled up and refiled and headed up Lake LaBarge (". . . on the marge of Lake LaBarge. . .") from Robert Service poem "*The Cremation of Sam McGee*" towards Dawson City where we were supposed to meet Stan Reynolds the next morning. He was already in town and found us as soon as we landed. Jess and Dorothy Taylor and Dr. Johnson from Boise had flown up on the airlines and would also be going in on the hunt. Jess wanted a mountain grizzly and Dr. Johnson was after white sheep.

The next morning we followed Stan Reynolds in his 180 taking them in. It was about 150 miles northwest to Stan's T.N.T. Mountain Camp. Mr. Taylor and Dr. Johnson would be going one way with a couple of guides, and Joy and I would be going with Stan Reynolds and another string of horses. Dick Hall and an Indian guide named Arthur Anderson would be flown out one at time in the Super Cub and landed on a ridge top to backpack hunt for sheep and grizzly. Stan got them both deposited but needed to air drop some more groceries to their campsite. He asked me if I would be the bombardier. Yahoo! He said he would wrap the groceries, including eggs, in a foam mattress and tie it to a ten-foot rope and he would fly low over a willow bush by their camp and I would let the package down and drape it through the top of the willows. It worked and when we saw them a week or so later, they cursed us out for breaking one of the eggs! Dorothy Taylor would stay with Stan's wife Ruth to visit and catch up on her reading. Dick got a nice Fannin (blue haired) ram on that part of the trip and got to see a wolverine.

Joy and Stan and I took some horses and headed another direction to hunt. I got my white ram about the third day, thirty-six inches but really heavy horns. Number 3 of my Grand Slam! I got a nice fifty-five inch Yukon moose a couple of days later and an old female mountain grizzly from that carcass a few days later. There was a white wolf trying to steal pieces of meat from the grizzly, but I couldn't get a shot. (I was going to kill the grizzly and swing on the wolf before he got away. It took three shots to anchor the grizzly and by that time, the white wolf was long gone)!

We went back to the T.N.T. Mountain to check on the rest. Dr. Johnson had taken a white ram, a grizzly and a wolverine and Stan took him out to Whitehorse. He flew out and brought Dick and Art back from the fly camp. They would rest a day and regroup to be flown over to the Porcupine River for a raft trip to the Alaska border for moose and grizzly. Stan and I spent a day flying to look for caribou and a grizzly for Mr. Taylor to hunt. No caribou but we flew by a moose carcass from a previous hunt and Stan could see a grizzly had been working on it. As we flew around the mountaintop, we flew by a narrow pass and standing upright in the pass was

Stan Potts and Dall ram from the Yukon. Stan Reynolds, guide and outfitter.

a very large grizzly. Magnificent sight! It was about one day from the ranch so one of the Indian guides took Mr. Taylor over to see if they could find the grizzly. They did, but the shot didn't kill the bear and they spent a couple of days trying to get the bear but to no avail. They came back and Mr. Taylor was very discouraged. He was over seventy years old and this was about his last big game hunt. He did go to South America twice for jaguar and was successful on the second try. Our hunt was over but I had ram Number 3!

I only needed my Stone Ram for my Grand Slam. I booked a hunt with Frank Stewart in the Cassier Mountains of Northern BC for August of 1974. Bill Kornell, Fay Detweiler and I flew north in a 185 that we borrowed from Robin Johnson over in Montana. (Bill's planes were busy in his flying service and mine broke down just before we were ready to leave). I came up from Wells, Nevada, and stayed all night with Bill in Salmon, Idaho. Our plan was to leave Salmon about 4:00 a.m. and fly all the way to Watson Lake in one day. If things worked right, you can fly a long way north and west as you gain some daylight. It worked and the next morning we got in a float equipped Beaver loaded to the gills with us, gear and supplies for Frank Stewart.

Frank's niece about eight years old sat on my lap, and I couldn't see how it would fly. We were definitely overloaded. The pilot went about two miles down the lake and started back into the wind. About every ten seconds, he would look out see if the floats had come out of the water any. He'd pull back on the yoke, gain a little on the front of the floats, push forward and gain a little on the back, rock it sideways, gain a little more. Finally, it lumbered off the water and he throttled it back a little as the engine had heated up to the red line. We flew back south to Tuya Lake where Frank and Ann Stewart lived year around. They had some cabins and Frank trapped beaver mostly in the winter. Ann had lunch for us when we arrived.

We then flew out to different lakes to start the hunt. Fay and I were flown to a lake called Nome Lake. Two guides had been four days getting

My 10 ½-year-old Stone ram.

the horses there, and it took us probably twenty minutes to fly over. Dan Stobbie, who now owns the bordering area, would guide Fay. They would take the horses around the backside of a mountain range. My guide Curt and I would take a canoe and row and portage a string of lakes and we would rendezvous a week later. When we landed, the guides had supper ready. The main course was an eight-pound lake trout they'd caught on a bent horseshoe nail and a piece of bacon!

Neither Curt nor I knew much about canoeing. (It's not a big means of travel in Nevada!) The first hour we sort of pawed our way around in circles before finally getting a system to work. The plan was to row an hour or so, pull in and glass the mountains and then move on. Also, the plan was to shoot something to eat. I had tags for mostly everything so practically anything that showed itself and was edible would be in danger from my .264 Winchester Mag. We had meat for only about three days so not only were we glassing the mountains for sheep, we were looking at the close mountains for moose and caribou. About the second day, we had pulled in to camp for the evening. Curt was setting up the tent, and I took the spotting scope and rifle and hiked to the top of a little hill about one-fourth of a mile away where I had a better place to look for sheep. Pretty soon I spotted sheep on the distant skyline. Every one I could find was skylined. I'd never seen Stone

On the Stone sheep hunt were (from left to right) Dan Stobbie, a guide; Stan Potts; Curt Skjonserb, a guide; and Fay Detweiler.

Sheep before but thought it was odd. One appeared to be a good one but it was a couple of miles away and probably 5,000 feet up. While I was watching the sheep and looking for more, I heard a noise in the brush patch to my right. It sounded like something coughing and grunting. I had no idea what it was but got my gun loaded and close by. About then, a bull caribou came trotting out about seventy-five yards away. I shot. He stopped, backed up, took off as before. I shot, he stopped, backed up, took off, three times exactly the same. I couldn't figure out what was happening. After the third stop and back up, he reared in the air and fell over. Soon after I got him, Curt came running up. He said, "After all the war, I thought you had been eaten by a grizzly!" (It's two demerits if the guide's client gets eaten by a grizzly)! I explained what had happened and asked him why the caribou wouldn't go down after being shot through the chest. His words, "They're so dumb they don't know they're dead!" So now we had some great meat to take on with us to the rendezvous site. In case Dan and Fay hadn't gotten any meat, we'd be okay for several days.

  I wanted to go to the top to look at the ram I'd seen. The sheep were still mostly in the mountaintops acting very nervous. We spent the day up there and never found anything but ewes and lambs. We were headed back down in the late afternoon when wolves stared howling about one-half mile below us. Now we knew why the sheep were acting so crazy! We started

Nome Lake, British Columbia, the locale of my 1974 Stone sheep hunt.

glassing and pretty quick could start seeing them. One big black one was lying down and howling. Curt asked if I wanted to shoot a wolf. "You bet," I answered. He said, "I maybe can't find Stone Rams, but I can call wolves." He told me to go down toward the wolves about a hundred yards and hide in the rocks. He would start howling and the wolves would come up the hill where I could open up on them. Frank Stewart told me he paid the guides $10 per wolf tail so I knew they weren't the most popular animal with the outfitter. I got hid out. Curt started howling. I peeked around my rock and here they came, including the big black one. The wind was still coming uphill. In a few moments, I could hear the shale clattering and knew they were getting close. Soon I could hear one going by my rock. I peered around and there was a wolf pup! I knew that as soon as he got by, he'd smell me and no more would show anyway. I shot him from about ten feet, jumped up and ran towards the others, but they were all out of range before I could see any of them. Not very proud of myself but rationalized I might have saved a few sheep in the future.

About the sixth day we pulled into the bank to have lunch and glass. We soon spotted six Stone rams about one and one-half miles ahead of us and 4,000 feet up on the mountaintop. One of them was really dark and looked pretty good plus this was the first probably legal ram we had looked at. We went to bed with him in the spotting scope and woke up the next morning with him still there! A good omen? I sure hoped so. It took us

The mountain where I finished my grand slam.

about four hours of straight up climbing to get near the top. It had started to rain, snow and sleet on us part way up. I was very wet from the perspiration and moisture falling on us. No way to get warm and the wind was really howling. It finally cleared, and we sneaked over to try and find the rams. A completely white ram jumped up and ran away from us! No sign of the other rams and I was just sick plus very cold.

We got over to the edge out of the wind a little bit where we could glass. After about an hour of trying to see through my shaking field glasses, I spotted a ram horn through the brush way back down at timberline. The rams had left the mountain top to get out of the wind. I was so cold I told Curt I had to go down and see what I could do before I froze to death. I got behind some rocks and started doing butterflies and pushups until I got my body warmed up where I could maybe hold a gun steady. I then started hurrying down the mountain until I was only a couple hundred yards from where the rams had been. I peered over and couldn't see any of them. Damn! What had gone wrong? I kept working forward and soon looked through a narrow crack in the ledge. The crack was about six inches wide and thirty feet long and at the end of it were the eyeballs of two Stone rams. I knew I was had, so ran out on top of them as fast as I could. When I got to the edge, the rams were lined out running full speed about 200 yards away. I sat down, got the gun on my ram, touched it off and missed! Jerked another in, tapped it off and I had my Stone Ram!

My Grand Slam was complete and for all time I will be the 160th person to have taken the four species of North American Sheep as recorded by the Grand Slam Club. The first Grand Slam taken by an Idaho born hunter. A dream come true for the farm boy from Idaho! Since then I have taken another Dall Ram in Alaska and a really nice Bighorn Ram here in Idaho.

Chapter 14

The *Life* Story

One year while we were at the Taylor Ranch, we were contacted by "Alcoa Aluminum Hour" to see if we could feed, house and take care of a television crew that would be doing a documentary. The series was one hour each on the four most famous *Life Magazine* photographers.

John Dominis was a wildlife photographer, and they would be filming him while he was filming wildlife. It sounded interesting to us plus a chance to make some money. They would be doing part of the series in other parts of the world including on the main Salmon River by boat. They were with us about a week. Joy cooked for them, and I packed them and the camera gear when they all went to the mountains.

Everyone was interested in our lifestyle, and they all said they should be doing a story on us. The following winter we received a call from Ann Hollister, one of the writers for *Life*, and John Dominis, saying that the powers to be at *Life Magazine* would like to do a story on us if we were interested. We decided yes and the arrangements started to unfold.

They had heard about the ranch in Nevada so they wanted to do part of it on our life in Nevada and the rest during hunting season at the Taylor Ranch. There would just be the writer Ann Hollister and Mr. Dominis. They came to the ranch in Nevada in the early spring so we weren't doing any farming. However, I was wintering 380 Charolais bulls for Dorothy Gallagher. One day I was going to move them to a new feed ground and John wanted to get some exotic pictures of the cowboying. He set up a tall stepladder in the center of the highway and filmed the bulls from above as they passed on both sides. I was greatly concerned for his safety because it was kind of like herding house cats and you didn't have complete control of the situation and these guys were somewhat larger than house cats! It worked without incident and they made plans to come to the Taylor Ranch that fall during the late hunts.

We hunted through Thanksgiving then, and some of the hunters always booked that hunt so they could get in on Joy's Thanksgiving dinner.

They wanted to participate in and witness Joy feeding 20 to 30 people in a tent. We always had the girls flown up from Nevada and they sometimes brought friends, so with hunters, guides, helpers, passersby, family, etc., we usually had pretty extensive participation in the Thanksgiving celebration. Also, the bighorn sheep would be rutting and John wanted to try for pictures of rams butting heads, etc.

They spent another week with us during this period. One thing I remember was John and I up on the hill taking sheep pictures. A nice ram was lying on a little ridge and I figured I could drive him right by John for some great close-ups. We got John a blind built and all situated, and I went to get around the ram. There were about six inches of fresh snow. Everything worked great, and the ram ran around the hill and right by John's blind. I figured he had some super ram pictures. Right? Wrong again. While John was waiting, he noticed the snow fleas on top of the new snow. I don't know the real name or what their purpose is in the order of things, but we call them snow fleas. They are about the size of medium ground pepper and black. I've seen them cover the snow like coal dust. Anyway, he put on a magnifying lens to photograph them, and when I got there he was looking down through the camera lens on a tripod. He had great pictures of snow fleas but didn't know the ram had run by within ten feet.

Anyway, after a few months, Ann called us and said the story was scheduled and gave us the issue. Just before that time she called again and said it had to be bumped because of some world crisis. A few months later, she said that it would come out in a special issue of *Life* called "The Marriage Experiments." We were in Fallon, Nevada, with our oldest daughter Kay at a high school rodeo when one of our friends came back with a copy she had bought at the drugstore. We had our pictures on the cover of *Life Magazine*! Pretty big stuff for a couple of kids from the boontules.

We were supposed to get a full set of all the pictures that John shot with us in Nevada and Idaho. However, *Life Magazine* went broke right after the issue came out. One story on the Pottses and an institution comes tumbling down! We did not get the pictures. So all we have are a couple of copies of the April 28, 1972, *Life Magazine*, and a check for $1.00 paid to us from *Life Magazine*, the memories of that unique experience and a letter from Ann Hollister saying that she was sorry but she couldn't retrieve our pictures.

The Life Magazine cover from April 28, 1972, with Stan and Joy Potts photo under the title "Frontier Partnership in Idaho" which was one photo story told in the magazine's special section on "New forms in a cherished institution" about marriage.

Stan and Joy Potts are a frontier-style team
PARTNERSHIP

The Life Magazine caption for this photo reads "In the cooking and dining tent, she (Joy Potts) laughingly comforts Stan Potts after he told a joke about himself.

Life Magazine caption: "Whacking away at the never-ending task of feeding five wood-burning stoves, Stan splits logs. It is Joy's job to whittle wood shavings for starting the fires."

The Life Magazine caption for this photo read: "In the organized shambles of the dining tent, the camp celebrates Thanksgiving – with the three Potts daughters flown in specially (left side of table).

Life Magazine caption: "In the center of their wilderness compound, Joy Potts hands out sandwiches and candy bars as the hunting party sets out in search of deer and elk."

Chapter 15

Trapshooting

We were living in Nevada and the Elko paper would come out with stories about the local trapshooters –"Elko Baby Grand Trap Shoot" – "Nevada State Trapshoot,"etc. I had always been intrigued by the game and decided that I would like to see what it was all about.

They had built a new trap facility at Spring Creek near Elko, Nevada, and had a shoot with Hollywood celebrities and nationally known trapshooters there to help publicize it. We were going to go, but I had a breakdown in my irrigation system, and we didn't get there until the shoot was over.

However, there were practice traps open so I borrowed a gun, bought a box of shells and a practice ticket and went out to a trap to try singles (16-yard targets I found out). I remember the puller and trap boy talking, "You won't have to keep score much; the guy has never shot before."

Anyway, I missed the first one. It surprised me! Then, I broke the next 22, missed the 23rd, and ended with 23 out of 25. I was basically hooked from that point forward and for the next fifteen or so years, I shot at most of the shoots in Nevada, Idaho, and sometimes the winter chain in Arizona. (Oftentimes wishing for that original 23 out of 25!)

You will notice the above miss of my first bird and the ensuing excuse? I was able after fifteen years to have been able to use the maximum number of excuses known to the trapshooting world. I found that after about the sixth time you miss and blame it on a slow pull by the puller the other trapshooters will tell you, "Just use the numbers." "Slow pulls are number 3!" "A bee got on my barrel"– number 8. "Dust in my eye" – number 4. And so on . . . .

My first big win came at the Golden State Grand in Reno, where I was lucky – YOU BET! – to break 98 out of 100 in the handicap and had played all the money. What that amounts to is that you bet on yourself against the others who play the money. You bet on each 25 birds, each 50 birds, plus the total score. I won over $2,000 and the "Trap and Field"

Magazine photo showed Stan Potts, who had headed all handicap shooters on the opening day of competition, with Linda Garrigus, who was the high D shooter in the opening 16s.

magazine interviewed me and had some pictures and a story with my score and several current and former All-Americans. Sure was a good feeling, plus it helped the old wallet!

    A highlight of this win happened to be the last bird, and believe you me, the pressure had built up. Our squad leader was an elderly gentleman from back east, and we had had problems all the way through with various things. Anyway, I was the last shooter and on post five for my last bird when the old gentleman starts to walk back to the scorer. I looked down at my gun with my last shell loaded and said to myself, "I sure hopes there are 26 shells in that box!" Anyway, the other shooters got him straightened out, and I called for my last bird. It was a screaming right, and I was sure there were six or eight birds, but luckily I hit the one that counted! The really odd thing about this story is that I had shot at Boise, Idaho, a couple of days before and had broken the WORST score of my life – 62 out of 100! I couldn't break one with a hammer and couldn't figure out what the heck was wrong!

    Another good shoot for me was the Elko Baby Grand where I won the High-All Around Gold Coin Buckle. One of the first persons to congratulate me was Ray Stafford, an All American and Olympic Champion – one of the ones whom I had beaten for the buckle.

Along in the middle of my trapshooting career, we were living in Hailey, Idaho, and my good friends, Ben and Peggy Hurtig, who operated the Sun Valley Gun Club had a shooting clinic with Dan Bonillas as the Instructor. Dan was one of the all time greats at all types of shotgun games and he was in his prime. Unfortunately, I had figured out a pretty good system and in trying to change to Dan's system, I got myself really fouled up. I couldn't hit a darn thing for about six months. I was slowly figuring out that the trapshooting game is approximately 98 percent mental. I got the army shooting manual and the Olympic shooting manual and studied them both diligently, especially the parts about how to keep negative thoughts out of your mind. I was then able to get my shooting back on track and much improved.

My last big shoot was in Boise, Idaho, at the Idaho State Championships. I averaged 97 over 800 birds and came within three birds of winning the State High-Overall Championship. I was a class B shooter and won the State Class B Championship by 28 birds. I was 80 straight in the Doubles as I went to the last trap where the birds were much higher than the other traps – I panicked (although I loved high birds). I had a

The lady in the center points to my 99 in the handicap category at the Idaho State Shoot in Boise.

mental lapse and missed four of the last twenty for a 96. I won my class again, but missed the State Championship by two birds. Still, I ended up winning a couple of thousand bucks so it wasn't a total loss.

My eyes were starting to lose some of their clarity so I haven't shot for several years. I would like to try it again sometime if I were to get my eyes fixed. I truly enjoyed the competition and the friends we made. No other sport that I can think of allows you to compete with the best in the world and gives you a chance to beat them.

The year I wrestled "Hector The Bear" we attended the Chicago Sport Show. In the booth, from left in hats, are Martin Capps, Ted Epley, Jack Nygaard and Stan Potts.

Chapter 16

Bear Stories – Hector

One year, probably around 1966, Joy and I and Ted Epley, Jack Nygaard and Martin Capps went to Chicago to run the IOGA booth at the sport show. The show in those days was held at the old Chicago stockyards. Adjacent to the convention area was the amphitheater, and there were shows and exhibitions going on nearly continually. One of the shows was Hector, the wrestling bear. He was owned by Tuffy Trusdale who had been a world champion wrestler. The bear was a black bear that weighed 500 pounds.

One afternoon I was on break from the booth (at the bar) when the guy that refereed the bear wrestling came in and sat down close by. One of the guys I was with was from Arkansas and his name was Sonny Dean. Sonny asked the referee, "Hey, when do we (note the *we*!) get to wrestle the bear?" The referee responded, "You really want to wrestle the bear?" Sonny replied, "You bet!"

Four or five days later after I had forgotten about Sonny's conversation, here comes the referee to inform me that we are up. It's Saturday afternoon and the biggest crowds of the week. The bear wrestlers rendezvoused at ringside for the instructions. The bear would have a muzzle over his jaws. You were to stand up with him with your hands on his shoulders to start the match. They were very explicit to not swing at or hit him. There would be about six guys lined up to take their turns. Might I add that no one had ever pinned Hector for three seconds.

Sonny Dean went first and was promptly disposed of. The second wrestler was from the Chicago Bear's football team and very little smaller than Hector. He was also somewhat inebriated. Hector promptly put him on the mat. The guy got up and took a swing at Hector. Hector dropped down on all fours, jumped out of the ring, swam the full length of the fly casting pool and headed up into the bleachers before Tuffy could get him under control. He brought him back and the next wrestler was a short, stocky outfitter from Wyoming. He spun into a Half Nelson and put Hector on the mat, only for a short second, I might add.

Smoky, one of our biggest black bears. With its hind feet on the ground, its nose was two feet above Joy's head.

Now it was my turn. I had Jack Nygaard as my manager. I thought to myself, "I'm a lot bigger than that guy from Wyoming. If I can get the bear's head down like he did, maybe I could hold him." Anyway, I slipped into my Half Nelson and ouch! My left arm felt like it was coming out of the socket. I looked around the bear's head, and my left wrist was in his mouth! Muzzle, yes, but not foolproof! He threw me over his shoulder to the mat and jumped on me. I heard and felt ribs breaking. It was two out of three falls and believe me, Hector had no problem with me on the next two falls! My manager Nygaard said that while this was going on, he looked up in the stands to see and hear Joy hollering, "Come on, Hector!" Yeah, four ribs broken.

Smoky

While we were outfitting in Chamberlain Basin, the bear population was pretty high and we were constantly having them tear up our camps. One night we arrived at our Quaking Aspen Springs Camp after dark and in a snowstorm. I couldn't believe my eyes. The tallest tent out of four was about three feet high. The bears had ripped the tents apart and crawled out on a pole that we had the food tied to. The pole broke and they had destroyed and eaten nearly all of the food. We got the camp sort of rebuilt for the night. The next morning, bear tracks all over in the snow. One was very, very big. I had a bear trap and decided to set it to see if I could catch one.

The first night, I heard the trap snap, but the bear had pulled out. Just hair and blood on the trap. The next night I reset it and heard it snap, and the bear roared. I went out with my flashlight and the 45/70 rifle. The trap was on a twelve foot long chain and the bear was up the tree at the end of the chain. My flashlight was very dim, but I thought I could see well enough. I shot and the bear roared, came down the tree and went back up. One of the hunters, Dr. Bob Range, was in a tent right by all of this. I hollered, "Bring me a good light!" The side of the tent lifted up a few inches and he slid the light out. I could see better now. Shot again. Same thing. Bear roars, comes down the tree, goes back up. Three times I did this and after the bear went back up the third time, he fell from the tree dead. I cleaned him that night and skinned him the next morning. One of the biggest black bears I have ever been around.

The Washing Machine Bear

At the Chamberlain Basin Camp, we had a lease on the Hotzel Ranch owned by the Idaho Dept. of Fish and Game. We were building a log cabin and had the roof on so we could use it some. The meat pole was behind the cabin in the edge of the trees. A bear moved in on us and was causing damage to the meat. I hung a lantern by the meat but the bear would stand in the shadows behind the elk quarter so I couldn't get a shot.

We had a bear trap and a twelve foot log chain, so I set it. However, I couldn't reach a tree to anchor the chain. We had an old Maytag washing machine so I pulled it over and hooked the chain to it. I figured I would hear the commotion and could go dispatch the bear. Didn't work. I got up the next morning and the washing machine and trap were gone. Also, two sides of my pole corral had all the poles broken. I woke one of the hunters, Don Hornaday, and asked if he wanted a bear hide. We started following the trail of washing machine parts down through the willows and soon found the culprit tangled in the willows. He was a beautiful brown color. As Don skinned him, I went back and rebuilt my corral!

The Hay Cable Bear

In our early years at the Taylor Ranch, we operated from tents set up in "Dave's Onion Patch." This was where Jess and Dorothy Taylor told us that Cougar Dave Lewis, the original homesteader, had his garden. Dave had come to the Big Creek Country as a civilian packer for the army in the Sheepeater Indian War of 1879 and had liked what he saw. He returned after the Indian fiasco and eventually homesteaded and proved up on sixty-seven acres in the creek bottom.

We had a bear visiting every night. One night in a horrendous rainstorm the bear dragged a bone behind our tent and was crunching away on it. I had my .357 Colt Python pistol and asked Joy if she would hold the light on the bear so I could dispatch him. Her words were something like, no exactly like, "Go to hell!" So, back to the bear trap. I made my set and baited it with a piece of honey covered meat. Dragged big poles and made a pair of wings to funnel the bear to the trap. Once again, my chain was too short to reach a tree. At the hay corral was a 100 foot cable that we used to roll the hay loads off the wagons and into a stack. I dragged the cable down, hooked it to a tree and anchored my trap chain to it. Fairly simple, eh? Negatory. I was pretty good at trapping bears but not so good at predicting the outcome.

When the bear sprang the trap, all hell broke loose. The bear roared and took off. Hit the end of the cable chain and roared. Headed another direction. Now, you have to realize that there were scattered alder and birch trees all over the area. I'm out there with my flashlight and pistol. I'd see the cable. There is a 50/50 chance that there is a bear on the end of whichever direction I go. I would find the bear; he would run. I would shoot; I would run. The bear would roar and after several of these sashays through the forest, eventually I had him secured. About then I saw a flashlight slowly coming through the trees. One of my guides, Fay Detweiler, and his wife Pat were sleeping on the other side of the creek and he had come to see what was going on. He said he was having a nightmare that one of the hunters had flipped out and when he heard the gunshots and roaring it fit right into the nightmare!

Next morning as I left with the pack string, I hollered back, "Joy, would you skin that bear for me?" Bad words again!

The Peach Tree Bear

Before we moved full time to Colson Creek we had started a small orchard with peach, apricot, cherry, apple, pear, almond and hazelnut trees. Some years when the berry crop isn't good in the high country, the bears come to the valleys and raise havoc with the fruit crop and can totally destroy the trees by climbing them and breaking the limbs and trunks

Our peach crop was on and nearly ripe when one of the bears adopted our place. He crawled over the fence and out onto one tree splitting the trunk close to the ground and totally ruining it. The laws had changed by now and you couldn't shoot bears just to protect your property. One night our German Shorthair, Shadow, growled and wanted out. As soon as he hit the ground, he headed for our best peach tree barking furiously. I went out the basement sliders and through the dog run with the shotgun and flashlight. I got about half way through the garden when a big black bear came down out of the peach tree and started to climb over the fence. Shadow grabbed him by the butt quite solidly and the bear turned and charged Shadow. Shadow came to me for protection.

I hadn't put any clothes on. Just my slippers and in my skivvies. Shadow and the bear made a couple more charges at each other when the bear went around me and into the dog run. Then I realized the dog run would funnel him to the slider doors in the basement, and they were open! I hollered to Joy to run down stairs and shut the door. She got there just in time to practice her karate chops at his nose and to slam the door in his face.

I ran up on the deck just as the bear got over the dog run fence. He headed down across the creek and I decided to fire the shotgun at his departing end to see if a little buckshot would keep him away. I'm not sure if I hit him but next morning I found I'd shot my water line full of holes!

The Telephone Bear

We had killed some elk at our Telephone camp and had the quarters hanging on a meat pole behind our tents. One morning I went to put the meat sacks on the quarters and found that a bear had visited us during the night.

That evening we made plans to try and remove the problem. I had two young guides, Larry Ledinsky and Jim Martiny, who wanted to kill a bear. We put their sleeping bags behind a log about fifty feet from the meat pole. We put tin cans filled with rocks on the pole so that they would fall and wake the light man and the gunner. I kept waiting for a gunshot all night as I couldn't believe the bear wouldn't come back. About 4:00 a.m., I got up to start the fire in the cook tent and put the coffee on. I walked out and shined a light on the meat pole. The cans were all on the ground and walked flat by the bear! I awakened my sleeping guides and showed them the damage.

The next evening my head guide and great friend, Dick Hall, and I decided we would sleep by the log. Dick would handle the light and I would shoot the bear. About thirty minutes after the last light went off, we heard the first can fall. Dick whispered, "Are you ready?" I whispered, "Yes!" Dick shined the light on the meat pole and there was the bear standing up

The telephone bear.

eating off a quarter of elk. I fired and the bear fell to the ground but was tearing around in a circle. I fired again and all movement stopped.

We went back to the tents and assured the guests everything was okay. Boone & Crockett president Fred Pullman and his wife, Robyn, and Peter Merlin and his wife, Betty, were on the trip and Pullmans' pointer dog Becky.

The next morning as we skinned the bear, we found one shot through the heart and one shot in a front foot along with an old slug embedded in a knee joint. Dick Hall's words were, "Boy, lousy way to kill a bear. You shoot him in the foot and when he sits down to lick it, you shoot him in the heart!"

Chapter 17

My Big Bighorn

The Idaho Fish and Game Department had transplanted some bighorn sheep into the Lost River Range near where I was born. In 1981 they decided to have a season and I decided to apply for a tag.

Now, I remember my dad telling me about a guy (my great uncle, Chris Carlson) he worked for who may have killed the last ram from the native sheep in 1934, the year I was born.

My grandmother had passed away in 1981, and I had honored her wishes by scattering her ashes from the airplane around the top of Mt. McCaleb that spring. The day of the sheep drawing, a friend of mine went to Boise to watch the drawing. I was at home that night when he called and told me I had drawn one of the seven tags for the first hunt ever in the Lost River Range.

I had about six weeks to scout. Every Friday after work, Joy and I would drive over so I could scout Saturday and Sunday. I would head into the mountains on Saturday morning and I would tell her where to meet me on Sunday evening. We did this every weekend. Plus, I would fly when the air was half way decent. I had a real estate business in Hailey, Idaho, and could leave when I wanted.

I had seen a total of thirty-three different rams, hiking and from the air, before the season and none that even started to get me excited.

The day before the season we drove to a canyon where I had seen four rams in the trees from the plane but couldn't get a look at them. I decided to start my hunt there, so I hiked up the night before the season. I found them the next morning. One was legal but not what I wanted.

My plan was to hunt systematically in one direction. I figured in thirty-seven days of the season I should be able to look at most of the sheep in the Lost River Range.

When I left Joy the night before the season, I told her where to meet me, if I was not back in four days. I hiked back into that camp on the

Big ram on the mountain, 1981.

afternoon of the third day, after only seeing the four-ram herd and three more small rams.

We decided to go to Mackay where we could take a shower and go out to dinner.

The next morning we went back to a canyon southeast of where I had stopped the day before. Once again, we picked a rendezvous spot if I wasn't back in four days, and away I went.

I was born and raised near there. I had hunted deer and antelope but had not been up in the country where the sheep lived. A lot of the country was plenty new to me.

I hiked up a long canyon toward the top. About noon I was resting and glassing when I say a couple of rocks near the top that looked a little different through the heat waves from the ordinary run of rocks. I decided to get a closer look. It took me about two hours more to get there. When I was able to get to a spot that I could see the country where I had seen the odd rocks, sure enough, they were rams, one legal and a two-year-old. But no go, again.

I was sitting in the shade of a tree at the timberline and glassing back a couple miles across a big basin. I picked up some sheep with the binoculars. I set up the spotting scope and, WOW, ten bighorn rams with three giants!

I slapped on my packframe and headed toward them. I figured I could get there by evening if everything went okay. I worked my way to the last ridge about three-quarter mile from the rams when they started off their mountain toward me. I didn't know what they were doing, so I just waited to see what happened.

The rams were going to water, but I didn't know that. I could have gotten right up on them in the narrow canyon where there was a spring. Anyway, I waited, and just before dark they appeared again, feeding back up the mountain toward where I had first seen them.

I unpacked my packframe and made camp under a green tree at timberline. I would be in sight of the sheep where I was, so to get towards a spot to start my stalk I planned on heading toward the bottom an hour before daylight so I could get out of sight of them.

I didn't sleep a wink. I just looked at the stars in all directions and thought of everything I could think of that could go wrong.

At first light, I was directly under the rams about 800 yards away. They got up and started to feed to my right, where there would be a chance for a stalk.

Scattering Grandma Coburn's ashes around Mt. McCaleb, where I killed the big ram.

The sun came over the top about 10 a.m. There was one small, lone Christmas tree about 100 yards below the rams, and a shadow from it came down the mountain to me several hundred yards. I decided I could crawl toward them in the shadow, undetected, so I started up. After about 100 yards, a small herd of deer came feeding by and one of the fawns decided I was something to play with.

He started bounding around me, bleating and making all kinds of commotion. Naturally, the ram herd became quite disturbed, so I just had to lay there. Finally, they all fed around the mountain, except the lookout ram. He just laid down and kept me pinned down until the fawn lost interest and went on with his mother.

The lookout ram went with the bunch out of sight, and I hurried around toward them. Pretty soon, I knew I should be pretty close when I heard lots of noise of shale clacking, and all the rams came rushing out of a little gulch and bedded down about 150 yards away!

The ram I had decided on was laying facing to the right but with a smaller ram directly behind him so I couldn't shoot. I was laying down with a small lupine plant about one foot high as my only cover.

It was now late enough in the morning that the downhill morning breeze was about to change and become an uphill thermal. I knew something would happen soon as the breeze was already blowing toward the

My big ram, 1981.

Joy and Stan Potts and the big ram.

rams in short spurts.

The rams started getting up of their own accord, but my ram and the one behind were the last to arise. He had only a few steps to be out of sight, so I got my gun on him, over my hand and steadied by my walking stick. The gun was wobbling so bad I could barely hold the aim on his shoulder. When the smaller ram moved, the big ram got up and was about a 45-degree angle away, so my target area was small. I shot, saw him stumble and the hair fly. Immediately he was out of sight.

I ran up to where I could see him following the herd, running to the left. I shot again and hit right under his chin. I reloaded and led him too much once more. I was down to the last shell in the gun, and the ram was going to be out of sight in a few feet. I said to myself, "Self, ya better learn you are leading him too much." I shot directly at his shoulder and down he came.

I went up to him and put my hands around the base of his horns and realized he was much bigger than I had thought.

I put two shells in the gun and shot two fast shots into the back of Mt. McCaleb, the mountain where I had scattered my Grandmother Coburn's ashes that spring. Two fast shots is our kill signal, and I thought Joy might hear it.

The ram was 39 6/8" long on the longest horn and 16 6/8" around the base. His green score was over 187 points, and after the sixty-day drying period it was officially 184 4/8". The biggest ram taken in Idaho for over thirty years.

I was very proud and felt very humbled that Diana, "The Goddess of the Hunt," had smiled upon me.

Two chip right and two chip left.

The Black Horn Ram.

Big bases, deep curl, good length – a fine ram!

Big ram within 200 yards of our home.

Centennial. This ram died in the winter of 1991; he had a score of 186 6/8.

Centennial.

Frank Church Wilderness, looking east down Papoose Creek and across the Bighorn Crags.

Chapter 18

Diary of 29-Day Sheep Hunt with 74-Year-Old Roy Bridenbaugh
Sept. 23 to October 20, 1983

Day 1: 9/22/83 – Met Roy at Andy Hagels about 10 a.m. Picked up last minute supplies to leave for Crags at noon. Had mix-up in signals and left without our packer, Mitch McFarland. Got to campground and met outfitter John Booker. Found we'd left Mitch, so I headed back to get him. Met him about thirty minutes back so turned around and went back to Crags campground for the night.

Day 2: 9/23/83 – Left at 8:30. Saw herd of ewes and lambs at Heart Lake. Made it to South Fork of Waterfall Creek at 5:30. Set up camp and cooked supper. Got into the first of the wonderful food Roy and his wife had prepared for the hunt (smoked turkey, pickled beets and eggs, homemade oatmeal cookies, fruitcake, etc.)

Day 3: 9/24/83 – Mitch left with the stock. We wouldn't see him again for 24 days. I packed my packboard for two- or three-day scouting trip. Climbed up and glassed Bobtail Burn. Some old tracks. Went up Bobtail and topped out on the Wilson Creek ridge. Saw one lone ram track. Camped on ridge after glassing 'til dark. Roy worked on camp (cut and split wood, dug out waterhole, fixed privy, built table, etc.)

Day 4: 9/25/83 – Glassed in morning. Finally headed up ridge and crossed over into Alpine Creek. Kept working up ridge and glassed to the head of Alpine and back across Wilson Creek. Passed three lakes. No sheep sign except old lone ram track. Came down ridge between South Fork Lakes to camp. Fish jumping all over the lake straight up above camp.

Day 5: 9/26/83 – Roy and I went up to the lake with fishing pole. I left Roy to fish – told him if I didn't return by 5 p.m. to go back to camp. I topped out across from Puddin Mountain. Worked east around head of four different canyons to Wilson Mountain. Few old tracks and beds. Saw twelve ewes and lambs on Puddin Mountain and in the pass going across above Buck Lake area.

Day 6: 9/27/83 – Rain and lightning storm all night. Fogged in in the morning so worked back down toward Grammers camp ridge to try to get out of the fog. Went back to camp in the rain. Eight sheep in Waterfall, six ewes and two small rams.

Day 7: 9/28/83 – Headed back to Bobtail Ridge. Glassed back toward Waterfall. Saw two big rams feeding around into Waterfall. Went back to camp. Roy and I packed up for five-day hunt. Left camp at 10 a.m. Took little tent to Waterfall and set it up. Left most of the gear there and headed around canyon to area I had seen the rams. Spotted one bedded in the shade on top of ridge. Too far around to make a stalk from above. Waited 'til sun went down and worked under them in a down wind but couldn't spot them. Went back to Waterfall camp in the dark.

Day 8: 9/29/83 – Went back to glass but couldn't spot anything. I finally went to top of the ridge in the afternoon and worked down to where I'd spotted them. Found their spooked tracks going back out of Waterfall. Backtracked them to find out what had spooked them. Found old smokejumpers camp and garbage with two yellow plastic bags tied in the trees that the rams had fed into. They had evidently never seen it before. I went back and followed them for about a mile. Gave up and went back to tell Roy the sad story.

Day 9: 9/30/83 – Raining hard so Roy and I went back to main camp, two and one-half hours. Rained all day.

Day 10: 10/1/83 – We had worried all the time on the last trip about bears, so Roy worked on bear-proofing as best we could in anticipation of our next chance at rams. He dug two pits – to bury our cooler in one and the apples, onions and potatoes in another. He built a ladder and put two strong poles up about twelve feet so we could hang the smoked bacons, hams and summer sausage in one and the metal pack boxes with everything else in the other, when we pulled out again. I went back through Bobtail to Rattlesnake Ridge. Glassed all along the way. Saw fourteen ewes and lambs in the little rough canyons in lower end of Wilson. Spotted four sheep that I couldn't identify because of rain and fog.

Day 11: 10/2/83 – Rained all night. Foggy in morning. Some glassing but not good. No sign except old.

Day 12: 10/3/83 – Came back to camp by the third lake. The one straight up from head of Bobtail. Glassed Waterfall. Now ten sheep with four rams. Saw lots of goats on this trip, mostly in Wilson.

Day 13: 10/4/83 – Took little tent and load of food to ridge by Grammers camp. Glassed Waterfall again. Now eighteen sheep with four rams. Largest maybe legal but small. Back to main camp.

Day 14: 10/5/83 – Roy and I hung and buried food. Left for Wilson Creek via little lake, five and one-half hours to top. Set up camp, and I went after water. Packed little wood camp stove from water hole.

Day 15: 10/6/83 – Roy glassed from rock. I went down ridge to glass mouth of Alpine. Worked around Alpine near the bottom up to near the head. Came out to top by Alpine Lake. No fresh sign. Glassed lots of goats again. Back down ridge to fly camp and Roy.

Day 16: 10/7/83 – Roy glassed and I went down ridge to top of switchbacks on Rattlesnake trail. Found Bob and Murts' camp from last year. Went down ridge toward Wilson. Found old miners' cabin and spring. Saw ewes and lambs but no ram sign. Saw five rams across river in Soldier Creek. They acted like they might be going to come down and cross over into our area. Went back and picked Roy up and we headed back to South Fork camp.

Day 17: 10/8/83 – Back to Grammers camp to glass. No new sheep in Waterfall. Up ridge to Puddin Mountain. No sheep, no sign. Saw good four-point buck. Went back down to camp by South Fork Lake.

Day 18: 10/9/83 – I left to go back and see if I could find the two big rams. Went straight across Waterfall and up ridge to top. Got pretty good look at the high basins on south side of creek and Puddin Lake. Couldn't spot anything so kept working down ridge toward where I figured the big rams were. Set up my tube tent and crawled out on ledge to glass. Spotted small legal ram at 5 p.m., feeding in trees. A few minutes later spotted two more. One borderline legal, the other well past legal but not big (young). It got dark so went back to my camp.

Day 19: 10/10/83 – Went back out on ledge at daylight. About 8 a.m. spotted one small ram and two big ones. They looked like the ones I had seen on the 29th, but it didn't matter because they were nice. I went back to my tube tent, dropped all the food and water that was left and headed back to the South Fork camp to get Roy. Arrived there at 11:45. We checked Roy's gun and found the scope was off. Sighted it in and hung buried food. Had a good meal and left at 3:00. Made Waterfall camp at 5:30. Decided to spend night there and leave next morning.

Day 20: 10/11/83 – Headed up ridge with Roy. Picked up and filled several water containers at small spring I had developed on way down. Made the top at noon. Roy was getting pretty tired, so I told him to get some rest and do some glassing. I went on up and out on the ledge to see if I could spot the rams. At 3:30 I spotted them and went back for Roy. It was borderline to have time for a stalk so decided to wait 'til morning.

Day 21: 10/12/83 – As soon as the wind got honestly blowing up the mountain, we moved in toward where I had crossed ram tracks going uphill. I told Roy I didn't think the big rams were in the bunch because the tracks were too small. When we got in on the spot and I had a chance to study the tracks, I realized that the big rams didn't have the kind of tracks they should have had (small). Anyway, I figured our scent blowing up the ridge had spooked them and could only hope they had spooked back into our area. Went to the top and, sure enough, they had headed over the top the right way. Spent the balance of the afternoon trying to locate them but with no success. After going back on the tracks, I found that the rams had split three ways. The smaller ram (which had been the largest ram with the herd of eighteen sheep) went back down with them. The four legal rams split into pairs with a big one and a smaller one in each bunch. One pair went down the ridge and one pair up it. We went back to our bags and packboards and made ready for the night.

Day 22: 10/13/83 – I headed back to the area where I had left my tube tent, food and water on the 10th to pick it up and see if I could figure where the rams were. I crossed pairs of ram tracks all over. On the way back I spotted the biggest ram of the bunch and his partner walking around a ledge down below me. they went into a group of fir trees at the base of a big cliff. This was at 1:30 and they didn't come out so I knew they had bedded. I went back and got Roy. We sneaked down to within 200 yards of where they were with the idea of waiting 'til they got up to feed so we could see them (too rough to safely try a stalk). At about 3:30, a fog bank dropped out of the sky and obliterated everything 'til nightfall. Went back up to our camp.

Day 23: 10/14/83 – Woke up to four inches of snow. Still snowing and fogged in. Decided it was going to be a wasted day. We were low on food and needed to get word out to our packer for a departure date. Decided Roy would go back to South Fork camp to get all the food he could pack. I would walk into the Taylor Ranch, about twelve miles west on Big Creek, to use their radio to get a message out for the packer to pick us up on the 20th. We would rendezvous at South Fork camp at noon on the 16th. I made it to the Taylor Ranch at 12:00. Finally got out to Joy to get the pick-up message to John or Mitch. Headed back down Big Creek and made the Bighorn Bridge at dark.

Day 24: 10/15/83 – Went to the university bobcat camp on Waterfall. Decided to see if I could get up the bottom of the canyon. Finally found old Indian/sheep trail through the ledges. There were ram tracks going up the trail only a few days old. After about a mile, the trail went by an overhand cliff with petroglyphs of an upright figure (Indian hunter), an animal that was obviously a ram, plus the usual hash-marks. I'm not sure of their meaning. I think they are some sort of calendar-game count or time spent at the spot, a diary. There was sand at the base of the overhand with the ram tracks in the sand. In a crack in the rocks about eye level was a vertebrae bone from a sheep-sized animal wedged back in the crack. It was a very mystical experience that I thoroughly enjoyed. I followed the rams on up to the top of the ridge after they left the bottom and they had left area 527-4. I really feel that these were the rams that I spotted across the Middle Fork at the mouth of Soldier Creek on the 7th. I think they were migrating to somewhere down the Middle Fork. On up the canyon I ran into a lone cow elk. Spotted three bulls across the canyon, one good.

Day 25: 10/16/83 – Roy made it in from South Fork with the last of our back-packable food. Decided he would take the easiest route back to the snow camp. I would go the shortest and fastest route for me, and we would meet at the same place we had left on the 14th. I would try to have something spotted. I picked up and filled all the water jugs which weren't quite so important now as we had snow to use for cooking. I set up the tube tents and went looking for the rams. I found two of them way below me, but close enough for a stalk that night. I went back to see if Roy had made it. He had just got to the campsite, but was pretty tired. Decided to try them next day. (Roy was totally bushed. I had to make decision I didn't like because of regard for Roy's well-being.)

Day 26: 10/17/83 – Headed down toward where I had last seen them. The plan was if we didn't spot them by the time we had gotten into the area where I had last seen them, then we would set it out until we either saw or heard them feeding. It was badly cut up country with lots of trees and cliffs. Roy and I split up about fifty yards apart so we could see better. I crawled down over fifty yards of rocks about the size of automobiles to a better vantage point. About 4:30 in the afternoon I spotted the biggest ram and his partner across the canyon and up near the top feeding in the edge of a large shale slide, approximately three-fourths of a mile away. I hurried back over the big rocks to Roy and in the process made some noise. I heard clattering rocks just below us as I got to Roy. He had heard them also and had started down toward me. Anyway, about 400 to 500 yards below us a pretty good legal ram appeared standing on a ledge looking back at us. Decisions, again. There we had a long shot at a fairly good ram. The big ram was on top in a good place to stalk and we had plenty of time to get there. After about a minute the ram jumped off the far side of the ledge and made one of our decisions for us. We could not see him anymore. Not too bad, eh! We still had the big ram to go after, right? WRONG! When the ram

Roy Bridenbaugh, 29-day hunt with no ram!

jumped from the ledge he made some noise and the big ram and his partner ran right out over the top of the mountain, without even looking back. They just ran away immediately. They were at least one-half mile from the other ram when this happened. Whatever had made these rams so jumpy had done an excellent job.

Day 27: 10/18/83 – Snowed all night and still snowing until afternoon. Decided to give it up and head back to get ready for our trip out. Made South Fork at 5:00. Mitch and John rode in at 5:30. One day early.

Day 28: 10/19/83 – Pulled camp and headed back. Crossed some ram tracks in the snow near the top above Barking Fox Lake.

Day 29: 10/20/83 – Back to Salmon.

On October 28, the severe earthquake hit central Idaho, rolling truck-sized rocks into the Middle Fork of the Salmon in this area. I believe the strange wild behavior of the rams was directly related to this impending quake that caused an estimated $2.5 million in damage in Custer, Lemhi and Butte counties.

I had nightmares about this hunt for months. That old man had saved his money most of his life to go on a sheep hunt someday. I kept wondering what I had done wrong. We were so close so many times.

"Ovis Ammon Darwini"

Chapter 19

Sculpting

My son-in-law, Jerry Black, had studied sculpting in college and was working on some pieces when we were at their house one Christmas.

I borrowed some tools and wax and immediately got hooked on trying to carve and mold something you could recognize (in grade school with clay, we had trouble recognizing my snowmen!).

After a few tries I felt like I was gaining, and I took a few pieces to Montana to be cast. It was quite expensive. Jerry built a kiln and furnace so we could cast our own.

One of my friends from Ketchum, Ted Werry who owned the Casino Club, had invested pretty heavily in silver bars when they were costing over $30 an ounce. He told me, "I'm getting tired of looking at those silver bars that are now worth $5 an ounce. Would you carve me a replica of the ram I killed in Mongolia, and then we will cast some in silver."

I carved one, and he asked me how much silver it would take and how much we would lose in each casting. I put the wax figure in water, figured the displacement, converted it to the weight of silver, and told him what I thought each would weigh. I also told him we shouldn't lose any silver. He evidently had an experience where part of the silver disappeared each casting.

We had never poured silver, and I remember as it got hot enough to pour that it spun in the crucible as it got near the top; other than that, it poured great. My estimate was within a few ounces on each piece, and I traded my work, cost, expenses, etc., for silver and cast pieces for myself that I sold. It worked out great.

Also, the people who had purchased the ranch we sold in Nevada, Dave and Pat Anderson, called and wanted to commission a sculpture of their herd bull, a Brahman. I gave them a price and received permission to sell copies on my own. I would personalize each one with the purchaser's brand and did really well with the piece.

I traded two of them to Pat Millington in Hailey for three nice Percheron mares that we trained to work, ride and pack.

I just seemed to get too busy with other projects (like five years building an airplane) and I haven't had time to keep the sculpting up. I plan on getting back to it someday.

"Second To None"

Stan Potts in a photograph that appeared in a 1983 newspaper article about his work as a sculptor.

"Day Money"

The pour – 2,000 degrees molten silver ready to go into an investment.

Left to right are "Day Money", "Destiny" and "Slim Pickins."

Chapter 20

The Lucky Shirt

The following three stories cover a time frame of probably five years. Each involved me and some of my horses. Each was potentially life threatening and in each situation I was wearing the same shirt! You tell me: lucky shirt or unlucky shirt? (Oh, by the way, I do have a couple of other shirts).

The first was in the early fall and I was back in the Stoddard Creek area of our present licensed big game area. I was setting up elk camps and had taken eight packhorse loads of camp gear to Cradle Creek and had spent a couple of days setting up that camp. In the eight packhorses were three colts (two and three years old, first major trip, two Percheron mares that weighed about 1,600 pounds). I had about four loads of tents and gear to take to set up my North Fork Camp. I was going to come back out to Colson Creek after I set up the North fork Camp so brought all the stock. I wanted to pack the three colts so packed them and one other with the tents, stoves, etc. I packed the little two-year-old mule Amos with a set of my metal pack boxes. They are very noisy and great to use in the training program, as they are nearly bomb proof and get the packhorses so that strange noises don't bother them. After that, they learn that strange noises don't hurt them. I'd just finished packing and was nearly ready to leave camp when a sudden hailstorm materialized. Well, you can visualize the little mule with the static din of the hailstones ricocheting off the metal box. The little mule broke loose and went careening around the area, bouncing off trees, knocking himself down and in a general state of panic. I went to the tent to get out of the hail and lay down and took a nap.

In about a half an hour, the storm stopped. I went out and found Amos, the little mule, with no major damage. I strung them together with four loaded ones in front and the four empties behind. I'd been out about an hour when I heard a major commotion behind me. I looked back and the string was coming toward me bucking and kicking and picking up speed. It was slightly downhill and a narrow trail. I was riding Banjo, very responsible and agile. I was standing in the stirrups turned half around and popping the leader Susy (one of the Percheron mares) on the nose and trying to get them slowed down. I figured I'd gotten into rattlesnakes or ground bees and at least with the bees, they come out on the fight after a few head had gone over them. We had picked up a fair head of steam by this time, probably a slow lope would explain it. About then Susy hit Banjo, spun him sideways in the trail and knocked us over the edge.

I pitched the lead rope back at the string and dived downhill and to the right of Banjo as we took our first flip. I got stopped pretty quick. I was on my hands and knees facing downhill and remember glancing out of my left eye as I was starting to get up and seeing Banjo getting to his feet to my left and downhill. I also remember my thoughts at that moment: "All right, we came out of this okay." A millisecond later I was hit in the back by a hurtling horse, knocked face down and then they started running over me stepping on my back, my legs, my ribs and my head. Somewhere in the wreck I remember trying to count horse feet. Let's see. Thump! Crack! Eight horses x four equals thirty-two feet. Ten or twelve feet have hit me. How many more can there be? Thump! Ouch! And then it got very silent.

I felt that I was very conscious the whole time but when I got to my feet facing uphill, Banjo was standing back up on the trail, probably twenty-five or thirty feet and there was not sign in any direction of my pack string. I hobbled up to the trail, quickly checked Banjo for visible injuries and could find none. Myself, on the other hand, hadn't fared real well. Blood was

Suzy, the mare I was leading in the Lucky Shirt No. One story.

running from the lower right rear part of my head, down my back and inside my pants and into my right hip pocket. My head was aching terribly, but I wanted and needed to find my pack string.

I was able to get on Banjo and start down the trail. I only went about 100 yards around the first bend, and there they were kind of tangled up in a big circle. No packs were off or slipped and there were no injuries that I could see. I untangled them and went on about a quarter of a mile to the North Fork of Stoddard where I would leave the main trail to head up it to the North Fork Camp.

By then the blood had stopped running out of my head. It was clotted with blood, hair and dirt. I tried to assess the damage, but it was all so numb I couldn't tell much. I could tell that there was a big cut behind my right ear but couldn't tell if my skull was cracked. Here I made a mistake, but I was still trying to figure out what to do. My options were like this: 1. Unpack, unsaddle and turn everything loose right where I was. This would guarantee the stock would be okay. 2. Take the stuff up to North Fork, unload it and then make whatever plans looked best then. 3. Just keep heading for the river with everything. (I was about five hours from the river).

Now to my mistake. I decided if I went to the creek and washed up my cut I could feel with my hand better what was wrong in there. I washed off, still couldn't feel much except I could put about three or four fingers up inside my scalp through the hole. But now, it had started gushing blood again and I finally could stop it only by wadding my handkerchief up and forcing it between my scalp and skull. I had aspirin and Advil with me but felt like I shouldn't try to mask the pain. I decided to head on up to the North Fork Camp and unload and then decide my next option.

I had traveled less than a mile when I had my first creek crossing. It was a steep downhill approach through overhanging alder and birch trees and on a left-handed (left slope downhill) mountain. Probably thirty yards down to the creek but brush so thick I couldn't see the crossing. Banjo stopped and I could see why. Across the trail were two down alder trees about ten inches thick, one about six feet in the air and the other about three feet. Here I was, no way to turn around and with eight horses perched above me and some of them with no experience at standing still in this kind of situation..

I had only one choice. I got out my hand saw about forty inches long that we have to pack at all times since the 1988 fire and started sawing. I had to make four cuts and let the logs drop so the horses could step over them. Probably took thirty or forty minutes but the string stood above me like they were carved in stone. I got back underway and had made it almost to camp.

Maybe three-fourths of a mile from camp but that last couple of miles is very steep. Susy, the gray Percheron mare, was giving out on me. She could only go a few feet and then a long rest for a few more. Decision time once more. I decided to unstring the ones behind her, lead her off the trail, tie up her lead rope and go ahead to camp with the rest. I hoped she would follow the horse tracks and smell after she had a good rest.

I went on to camp, unpacked and turned those seven horses loose so they could get to water and grass. But, no Susy. I took Banjo and went back towards where I had left her. She had started to follow, but a pretty good game trail that left the horse trail on a switch back on a level grade looked more inviting to her. I followed the horse tracks about a half a mile, found her and got her back to camp. I unpacked, unsaddled and turned her and Banjo loose to go with the others.

As always happens to me after an injury of this severity, I went into shock. Uncontrollable chills, nausea, etc. I got my sleeping bag unrolled and with all my clothes and boots on was able to get into it and combat the shock as best I could.

I lay in that bag for at least two or maybe three nights and days. I was so stiff and sore and head still aching that I could not stand up. On the second or third morning, I was able to crawl out and get to my feet. Many ouches! I tottered up the hill, caught Banjo and a couple others and brought them all down to the saddles. I saddled them all up and headed for the river. I made it without incident and got them unsaddled, in the corral and fed.

I went over to a neighbor's, Joni Stark, to have her see if she could tell me more about the cut in my head. My headache had subsided by then and I was feeling a lot better. The scalp had gone back together pretty good so I decided to not go to a doctor. I still have a horse track scar there. Lucky shirt #1?

Lucky Shirt #2

The second incident involved Banjo and the shirt again. I had a sheep hunt up the Middle Fork of the Salmon River in the Soldier Creek area. I'd hired a guy to go with me to wrangle and he was going to meet me at Meyer's Cove where I would unload the horses. Just before I left, he called. His wife had broken her leg and he would not be able to come. I got on the phone to try to find a helper but had no luck. I called a pilot friend of mine, Frank Giles, in Challis and told him to find me a helper and fly him into Bernard Creek as soon as possible. I'd go in and scout for sheep and check Bernard Creek Airstrip every morning.

About the second morning I was at the Bernard Creek Ford on the east side across from the strip. Right after daylight, I heard Frank's plane. I saddled Banjo and Andy and forded the river. The ford is not very good with big, slick rocks and water probably thirty inches average depth. Frank had not found anyone and had flown in to let me know. He would keep looking and would come back the next day. He took off and I headed back across the river leading Andy. We were about three-fourths of the way across when Banjo fell sideways down river with his feet upriver. I got away, was part swimming, part walking down river. Banjo had no way to get his feet to ground and it was very hard to keep his head out of the water. When his head would come out, he would virtually scream.

I would grab his head or reins and try to spin him around and then lunge downstream to get away from him. I didn't realize, but we had gone quite a ways downstream and the flow of the river had taken us back where we were closer to the airstrip side. About the time I got him spun around, I also realized I was about out of gas. I swam to the west side and was barely able to pull myself part way out of the water. When I could look back, here came Banjo following me and Andy following him. We were just above the start of rapids and deep water at the bottom of the ford.

It was probably around 7:00 a.m. and 25 degrees and Banjo and I were totally wet. I got up and caught them when they came out of the river. I led them up to the picnic table at the lower end of Bernard Airstrip. I got

some wood, got my waterproof match kit and pitch stick out of my pocket and got a big fire going. I stripped out of my wet clothes and for the next couple of hours, led Banjo around the fire. I built a tripod of sticks and dried my clothes. We had both dried out before the sun came up. I decided I'd had enough of the river and rode up and around to cross on the Flying B Bridge. Frank brought me a helper the next day. Lucky Shirt #2? Oh, I didn't find a ram for the hunter and he beat me out of $1,650. He knows who he is so I won't mention his name.

Lucky Shirt #3

The third incident was crossing the North Fork of Papoose Creek. I was riding Dusty and leading six head. There were two hunters ahead of me and we were heading for Whiskey Springs where I had a camp and other hunters and helpers. The crossing here is fairly good but just across, the trail turns 90 degrees downstream and then about eight feet of slick rocks. The water was a couple of feet deep and the creek about four feet below trail level.

I had watered Dusty and was watering the string, but Dusty was in the slick rocks. He was impatient and trying to follow the hunter that had gone ahead. I had my head turned to the left watching the mules get a drink and then move up so a couple more could drink when I felt Dusty slip. By the time I could see what was happening, we were gone. He was probably horizontal. I dived out and away from him into the rocks and water. Once again I thought, "Alright, you got away!" Crack! The world fell in on me. Dusty was right on top of me and my head was under water.

I have lost three good friends to drowning in almost the exact situation and their faces were flashing through my mind. I couldn't tell whether Dusty had flipped clear over or if his back and the saddle end were on my shoulders. When he would lunge, it would take a little weight off my shoulders and I could get my head out and scream, hoping the hunters would hear me. In probably a minute of this I was able to pull myself out from under him and crawl to the far side of the creek and out of the water.

In a few minutes, I was able to get up. He was on his feet and I got him on the trail and in front of the string. I was once again totally wet, glasses broken, field glasses full of water and lots of "ouches" once again, but nothing major that I could find. About then one of the hunters came running back down the trail to see what was wrong. I told him of my wreck and what we had to do.

Once again it was cold and a pretty good wind. No place to get the string off the trail for about forty-five minutes. We went on up to a ridge top and I once again built a big fire, stripped down, tripod for the clothes to hang on, and I led the horse around the fire till we dried out. We still had about three hours to go and I was pretty stove up when we got there but was able to go the next day.

Everyone, after hearing these stories, told me I better get rid of that shirt. I, on the other hand, felt that I should have it sewn to my skin. I had come out of three potential catastrophes alive and kicking while that shirt was on my back. The next time I looked for my shirt it had vanished from my closet. No one will fess up as to its demise. But good news! I have put another shirt to the test at the end of the millennium and may be on the way to another lucky shirt!

For two or three years prior to this wreck with Dusty I had very bad pains in my neck and couldn't turn my head to look at the string without turning my body in the saddle. I went to a doctor and had it x-rayed. There were bone spurs around the spinal cord and several doctors recommended against an operation because of the danger.

A month or so after the wreck I caught myself turning my head with no pain! THE CRASH IN THE ROCKS WITH 1,200 pounds of horse on my back had broken the bone spurs loose!

Bobcats and Mustangs

The following two stories show how easy it is to get in trouble with a lariat rope.

I was bringing my cows and calves back from the lower place while we were ranching in Wells. It was hot and dusty and the calves were lagging back so I was heeling them as we slowly moved along through the greasewood and sagebrush. All of a sudden, the cows spooked and were scattering in all directions. Through the dust and running towards me was a bobcat. I had a loop built and as he ran by me on the left side, I put a California loop out and it settled around his neck. I was riding a young horse named Goucho and he was not overly thrilled about our catch.

Bobcats don't just hang on the end of the rope. They bound around somewhat. In one of the sashays, the bobcat grabbed Goucho by the left hind leg and we made some pretty wild tracks getting unraveled from that one. Finally, I got the rope wrapped around a sagebrush with the bobcat tangled up pretty tight. I went down the rope to get the loop off when I thought, "Hell, nobody is going to believe me unless I produce some evidence!" Herein, my plan unfolded. I would get my Levi jacket off the saddle, wrap the bobcat up tightly in it and wrap the rope around everything to keep my package secure. I figured I could keep his head out and he could get air, as long as I kept the feet in. It was nip and tuck getting on Goucho with my package, but it worked and I headed after my cattle herd. I caught up and we had about three miles to go to the house.

Every so often the cat would sort of explode trying to get his feet out and I would have to squeeze him pretty tight to maintain control. I finally got the cows to the fields and headed to the house to show off my bobcat. When I got there, he had died. I guess the stress and me having to squeeze so hard had choked him. I felt bad and would have turned him loose if I had known the final outcome.

The Mustang and the Snowmobile

My next fiasco with the rope involved my snowmobile and a mustang. I was checking canyons for lion tracks near Currie, Nevada. It was a snowy winter and snow was two or three feet deep on the valley floor. The mustangs had been forced out of the mountains and onto the flats to forage for grass. I came down into a wide canyon and there were about twenty head of mustangs below me. I gunned the snowmobile and headed them off so that they were running parallel to the mountain. I had seen Bill and Kay Lear heading out mustanging with their horses that morning. I figured if I could run this bunch around to meet them they could handle them and get them down to their corral. It was around eight or ten miles to their ranch. This was before Wild Horse Annie was able to get laws enacted to prevent the rounding up of wild horses. They were overrunning the range lands and needed thinning out.

I moved the herd a couple miles but was having problems keeping them together. Some were getting tired and hanging back and the leaders were trying to cut up into the hills and safety. Soon afterward, the leaders got ahead of me and split the bunch with eight head of stragglers that I could handle. I moved them on a couple of miles and spotted the Lears below me. Bill rode on toward the ranch and Kay unsaddled and stood by his horse so the mustangs would see his horse and come to him. They did, and he turned his horse loose to head for the corral. Remember that none of this was pre-arranged. I followed them with Kay on the back of the snowmobile. One two or three year old stud was getting tired so we had to leave him. Took the others right to the corral behind his saddle horse and with Bill helping.

I figured I could go back and haze the lone stud down. He just kept breaking around me and heading back. Therein hatched the new plan! I had my lariat with me as usual. I ran the tail of the rope down through the foot rest and up to the side with the throttle so I could swing the loop with my right hand and rope the stud, run the throttle with the left – run by him – pull him down – and tie him before he could get up. Is that a great plan or what?

Here is a hand painted picture of what happened. He broke back. I ran up behind him, stood up and roped him. He planted both front feet in a dead stop and kicked over his head. I couldn't stop and drove right under him. He came down on top of me and the snowmobile, kicked the windshield right off and he was mad! His teeth were bared, trying to grab me. Luckily, in the ensuing melee, the rope came off, as I had never been able to jerk my slack.

I gunned the snowmobile and got away from a very mad mustang stud. I went back, got my mangled hood and broken windshield, coiled my rope and returned to Currie very glad that old snowmobile didn't decide to quit about the time I was making my escape!

The Grizzly Charge

One year Ken Smith, Bill Kornell and I went to Alaska on a hunting

The grizzly charge. Note the fingernails on that dude.

trip. By going at the beginning of the season in Alaska, we could be back to get ready for hunting season here. Bill guided for me plus running his flying service and Ken was a neighboring outfitter.

We left Salmon at 4:00 a.m. about the first of August in my Cessna 206 – 8647Z. We took all the seats out but three so there would be room for one person to lie down and sleep. That way, Bill and I could trade off on the flying and if we didn't get hung up in weather, we could make it to Northway, Alaska, in one day.

We checked through customs in Penticton, British Columbia, and I flew from there to Watson Lake via the trench. We fueled up and Bill took over to fly to Whitehorse. I lay down and slept about an hour and a half then sat up and looked out. I didn't recognize any of the country from previous trips so asked Bill where we were. He said he was having trouble picking up Teslin radio. I said, "Are we north of the highway or south?" He didn't know. Then, under a fogbank directly ahead, were many glaciers coming down out of the fog. Also, a big lake and a small town. I laid out our map and drew a big arc for about one and one-half hours flying time. It intersected Atlin, B.C., which was a long ways south of where we should be. I figured the course to Whitehorse as 10 degrees and told Bill to get all the altitude he could so we could extend our flight plan. In thirty minutes we were badly off course again. Then we realized our compass deviation was so bad as to make it unusable. We flew by dead reckoning and followed the river to Whitehorse and with finger on the map on to Northway and customs again. After customs and buying our hunting licenses and tags, we flew back south to the Yukon border. We would land on the highway at Matt's place. He would take us to a lake about a mile away to meet Urbon Rahoi with the floatplane to take us to Ptarmigan Lake Lodge.

Matt had left Anchorage about 1927 because there were too many people. He hiked to a spot he thought was the furthest from anyone and built a cabin. He ran his trapline and did a little prospecting, happy as a lark, and then – they built the Alaska Highway right in front of his door! He figured then if you can't beat them, join them and he built a store, motel and gas station. Out front was the only "three holer" outhouse I have ever seen.

When we got settled at the old lodge (he was just starting a new one), Rahoi told us about the grizzly bears tearing up the lodge. He had trapped one but it pulled three toes off and got away. He had driven several hundred twenty-penny nails in a sheet of plywood and put it upside down by the window to the pantry. A bear had left tracks all over the bent nails and torn in to ruin things again. When they would leave, they would go through the plate glass windows and scatter glass clear to the edge of the lake. Naturally, he was pretty mad at the bears and wanted all guides and hunters to see if they could get the ones anywhere close to the lodge.

We took one of his Cushman Tracksters back about one-half day into the mountains and set up a little tent at the forks of two creeks. The next morning I took one ridge and Ken and Bill another. I wasn't seriously hunting anything but caribou. I had my camera, telephoto lens, tripod, etc., plus my .264 Winchester Mag. I found a lot of sheep and spent the day taking pictures and looking for a good bull caribou. That afternoon I came around the top of the hill where I could see back towards our camp. Glassing to see if the others were back yet, I spied a grizzly right by our camp. My first thought was that he had destroyed our camp and food and we would have to go back for more supplies. The bear was coming up the valley so that I could drop off the mountain and intercept him. While trying to get down, I got rimrocked and the bear went on by. A little ways further, he moved up on the other side of the canyon and laid down on a big rock the size of a boxcar.

I was about one-half mile away when he jumped up and went back into the bottom out of sight. I hurried in the direction he had moved and was pretty winded when I saw him across the canyon and above me. I had the telephoto lens mounted and set up the camera to take one picture while I was resting. I lay down and held on the top of his shoulders for the first shot. I figured the range about 400 yards. He spun around and bit at his shoulder

This photograph of four generations of the Potts family was taken about the time the lucky shirt was keeping me alive. From left in the back row of the photo are Stan Potts, Joy Blume Potts, Marion Blume and Jay Black. In front, from left, are Robyn Maxfield, Addie Maxfield and Tim Maxfield.

and roared so I figured I'd hit him solidly. I shot thee more times and the exact thing happened each time. I couldn't believe he kept going. He was moving around the canyon head above me and went out of sight right after the last shot. I immediately reloaded and as I put the fourth shell in, I heard something, looked up and here came the bear directly at me and full bore probably twenty yards away. I shot and there was no indication of a hit. I immediately shot again as he was probably about twenty feet and would be on me in a couple of jumps. He slid toward me and I ran to the left to get above him. I put two more shells in and looked down toward him with my finger on the trigger. There was no reaction as I touched him. He was dead. I looked at his feet and there were the nail holes in all four feet. One of the troublemakers would no more tear up Rahoi's lodge.

When I skinned him, there were only two bullet holes, both in the front. One, the first, had gone in below his chin and destroyed the heart and lungs. The second, that probably saved my life, had broken his neck right in front of the hump. When I got to camp, there was no sign of the bear being there. When the guys came in and I told my story, Kornell said, "I suppose you didn't get any pictures of him charging you!"

The reason the bear would roar and bite his shoulder was that it was further than I thought. When I'd shoot, I'd hit the shale under his chest and the rocks would explode up and bite him. I'd killed my first grizzly in the Yukon, but that was nowhere near the excitement of this one!

Chapter 21

Idaho Sheep Hunt
September, 1989

By Dan Pocapalia

Inasmuch as this was my 16th sheep hunt during the past ten years, I felt somewhat confident, even though some of my previous hunts had been unproductive and some were disastrous. With everyone's help and consultation, I selected who I considered to be the best sheep guide and outfitter in the state of Idaho, Stanley Potts from Hailey, Idaho, to serve my special needs, and, in turn, he selected the area that offered the best opportunities for bagging a ram in the 180 plus scoring range.

Stan picked me up on schedule at the Hailey airport three days before the opening of the sheep hunting season on September 2nd. Since my special permit allowed me to hunt any areas that were legally open to sheep hunting, I left it up to Stan to select the area that would offer the best opportunity for locating a ram that would score 180 plus. By any stretch of the imagination, this was a big order, but Stan felt confident that area 537 would be the right place to hunt, where only three permits were issued this year, and, as I understand it, the area had only been open for hunting the last four years, thus allowing the rams to mature to ten to twelve years old, for larger trophies with sixteen-inch-plus bases that are needed for a high score, and we both agreed on this. The weather was extremely hot, dry, and windy upon my arrival.

I had never met Stan Potts prior to his picking me up at the airport, and frankly, I wondered every now and then just how my blind date with a new outfitter was going to turn out. There's always a degree of speculation. During the two-hour drive to our camp site we talked about many subjects. I was really getting the feeling that I had made a good guide selection with a first class operation. It has been my experience over the years that the first sight of your camp can have a lasting impression and, to say the least, sometimes a big surprise, and not a good one.

Stan was carefully maneuvering his 4x4 up a narrow logging road when he finally announced, "We are there!" What I saw was a small meadow with foot-high grass, four horses grazing in the meadow, with a small igloo tent set on the far side of the meadow. I finally located the main, or cook's tent (the most important one), or what appeared to be the main tent. It was a mess, either it was never set up properly, or the wind had blown it almost down. Stan stared in disbelief and embarrassment. I looked at him and he looked at me and neither one of us said a word. He walked to the tent and opened the tent flap. Everything was scattered all over the floor. My first impression of our new camp left much to be desired. Stan assigned me the igloo tent and after forty-five minutes of getting my things organized, I joined Stan, who had made a complete survey of the tent situation. He concluded that the grazing horses had gotten tangled in the guide ropes that held the cook's tent up, and once the guide ropes were broken loose from the anchoring stakes, the tent collapsed – this made me feel much better. After forty-five minutes he had the tent in tip-top shape.

It turned out to be a great camp. The camp was dry and all water was brought in from a spring some miles away. The camp site was situated at an elevation of 8,800 feet, based on my altimeter, just a few feet below timberline.

The next two days prior to the opening of the hunting season were spent scouting and glassing different areas, especially mountains one to five miles away. We located many rams, but none were in the Boone and Crockett category. I also got the impression that Stan was toughening up the "dude" to see what I could handle at an elevation of 10,000 feet. I don't mind admitting there just wasn't very much oxygen at that elevation, but after a couple of days, I managed quite well. (I had passed my annual physical examination.)

On opening day we located four legal rams, none of which met my requirements. On September 3rd we were working a high, barren ridge well above timberline. The ridge consisted of flat, sharp-edged shale covered with frost. Stan looked down into the bottom of the canyon and located three rams feeding. We instantly lay down on the frozen shale so that our outlines would not be silhouetted on the skyline and immediately tried to determine if one of the two legal rams would make the book.

For eight hours we were pinned down in the one spot with the rams 1,500 yards from us. They would feed for a short period of time, then lie down. There was no way to backtrack out of sight, so there we were. We even went through the learning curve of urinating safely while lying down – which is a very, very tricky maneuver.

One of the rams was a possible Boone and Crockett "keeper," but he was too far away to determine if he would make the book. We both

Idaho auction tag holder Dan Pocapalia and outfitter Stan Potts on the last day of their hunt. Last day, last chance – no ram!

expressed our doubts and estimated that he would score 175 to 178 maximum – not good enough, but felt we would like to take a closer look at him. Finally, in late afternoon, we managed to back away from the rams' line of vision without spooking them.

The game plan for the next day was to attempt to locate the three rams, make a sneak close enough to make an accurate estimate of how he would score. We had preestablished that I did not want to bag a ram unless he made the book, since I had several in the 175 to 178 category.

At 6:00 a.m. the following morning, we were worming our way up the trail we named "Shoe Goo," because after several days up and down this steep shale mountain, our boots were coming apart and were in need of repair with the stitched seams coming undone, as well as the soles. I just happened to have a tube of "Shoe Goo" that saved the day. We both managed to repair our boots with this stuff.

Once on top of "Shoe Goo Ridge," Stan quickly located the three rams that we had seen the previous day. Stan suggested that we start our stalk immediately. The rams were several miles down the mountainside feeding on a small, rolling plateau. We figured it would take us several hours to get to the approximate area where Stan guessed they would be, for final inspection at, hopefully, a close range.

We were on our final leg of the stalk and had just crossed this large, flat meadow and worked our way up a low, flat bench with gently sloping plateaus. As we topped the bench, we paused for a breather and, once again, agreed that the ram must score 180 plus or it was a no go. Stan started to brief me, "Now, Dan, remember in Idaho, that if this is the ram we are looking for, you must be prepared to shoot at 400 yards or more." We concluded that I must aim six inches above where I expected the impact. Stan then asked me, "Dan, can you handle it?" I replied, "No problem. With my five pound, .284 smokestick, I can handle it." I was psyched to

Idaho Governor Cecil Andrus signs the first Idaho auction sheep tag. Joy and Stan Potts are standing just to the left of Andrus.

aim six inches higher; this was going to be the longest shot of my life. Stan said, "Now, get your smokestick ready; we will cross the shallow gully and once we crest the ridge on the far side, we should be able to see the rams. Let's go!"

I was all psyched up hoping that the ram would make the book. Stan said, "Don't shoot unless I tell you." We took ten steps and Stan tapped me on the shoulder and pointed down the shallow gully and there the three rams were, looking straight at us, very nervously, 40 yards away. I went down on one knee for a better gun rest, but I couldn't see the rams because a small ridge was impairing my line of sight, so I stood up in full view of the rams. At this point, I was positive that the ram would not score over 178. Nevertheless, he would be a respectable ram for any sheep hunter. Stan never uttered a word of confirmation that the ram would score 180 or more, and at that point, I just instinctively squeezed the trigger at the super close, easy shot. Even though it was made offhand, standing up, believe it or not, I just flat-ass missed that ram. I did not want the ram, and I was very disappointed that I missed an easy shot, but happy since he would not have made the book. My final conclusion is that he was just too close. I must have aimed six inches high and missed. It was a storybook stalk.

Several days later Stan spotted a ram late one evening that I was convinced would have made the Boone and Crockett record book. However, it was too late to make a stalk that night and we decided to try for him the next day. We spent the rest of my hunting days looking for him, but never saw that ram again. Keep in mind, that the smart ones live to grow those trophy horns; the dumb ones are hanging on someone's wall. During my ten-day hunt we located 25 legal rams.

This was sheep hunting at its best! At this point, I have no definite plans to return to Idaho for another hunt, but would give the possibility some consideration, if a good ram were located.

My grandad's saddle, one of my proudest possessions. It was made by famed saddle maker Frank Meanea, whose career spanned an era from 1868 to 1928. Meanea, who was the successor of the E.L. Gallatin and Company saddle makers, made a wide variety of riding equipment and was among the most popular saddle makers of his time. Among those he made saddles for were cowboy artist Charles M. Russell and author Owen Wister (The Virginian), notorious range detective Tom Horn and the legendary Buffalo Bill Cody.

Chapter 22

Reflections on Life Insurance

I remember my folks telling me that Grandad Gray was not a believer in any benefit of having insurance, except to the company. I think he was pretty well right.

Through the years, I had paid into and for several small life insurance policies, borrowed money on them to invest in two dry oil wells in Utah, and then paid the loans back.

A life insurance salesman talked me into cashing them all in and buying one large policy that would pay off as an annuity while we were alive and still have the face value. After about seven or eight years the company went broke, and we lost it all. Grandad was right, at least in this case.

Grandad's Saddle

I am in possession of several historical treasures – most notably my grandfather Herb Gray's saddle and a tree that has grown around a beautiful set of bighorn ram horns.

The balance of this chapter will be mostly old family pictures from both sides of my family – the history of grandad's saddle and the ram tree story.

You can't read the stamping on the saddle skirt any more but when my dad started riding it after granddad died, you could read "F.A. Meanea–Maker–Cheyenne Wyoming Territories."

It is on an eighteen-inch "Mother Hubbard" tree and as near as I can tell, it was made around 1880. I don't know if grandad had it made – or if it was bought new, used or whatever. What I do know is that he rode it till he died in 1942. My dad rode it until about 1965, and I had it relined and rode it a lot and used it in the hunting camp for the "big guys" until I retired it in 1994! It's still very comfortable and in great shape! How many saddles about 120 years old can you grab off the rack and go riding?

Stan Potts and Grandad's saddle.

This tree that grew around a bighorn ram skull and horns was cut down in the Lemhi Mountains of Idaho in 1940. The tree had 170 growth rings, which means it probably germinated about 1770, prior to the Revolutionary War. It is not known for sure when the bighorn skull was hung over the tree's limb, but conjecture has raised several possibilities. If the tree was 35 years old when the skull was hung on its limb, the incident would have occurred about the time of the Lewis and Clark Expedition's trip through the area in 1805. If the tree was about 65 years old when the horns were hung on its limbs, it would have taken place about the time of the fur trapping era in the region. A coffee-table size reproduction cast of the historic find was made several years ago by Rick Alkire of H.O.R.N.S. Inc. and numbered, limited edition castings in two sizes were made and are for sale.

Stan and Joy Potts home about the time its construction was about complete.

A thunderstorm brewing in the mountains, a view from the deck of our home.

A view at night of a forest fire coming toward our house.

A helicopter firefighting crew is shown dipping water from the river by our house in an effort to stop the fire, which was racing towards our home.

Chapter 23

Some Stan Potts Poetry
"Remembrances"
Idaho Outfitters 2001 poetry contest

Trying to write a poem is a daunting task, I find.
First, you have to pick a story, then get a title in your mind.

Already I'm in trouble 'cause I can't pick one to enter.
It will burst my poetry bubble if I can't get this thing off center.

I've gone through the options of the many different ways to go.
Like the old-timers in this business that rode the trails so long ago.

Most are gone, but not forgotten – each a legend in his time.
And on the trails that we're still riding – we should keep them on our mind.

For time is but a wisp of wind in the history of these guys.
And just to survive in the times they did proves they were more than wise.

There's Cougar Dave, Frank Lantz, Sandy Brooks, Louie Ribellet, and Jess Taylor, Al Tice, Shorty Derrick, Gerald Twitchell, Marve Hornback, Ray Seal, and Paul Filer, Jack Nancolas, Verl Potts, Bill Guth, Eddie Bennett, Bill Sullivan, Larry Garner, Leo Jarvis, John Gillihan, Andy Anderson, Pat Reed, Bill Watson, Dan O'Conner, Don Habel, Joe Zonmiller, Gertrude Maxwell, Bob Cole, Ken Wolfinbarger, Archie McCarthy, Lafe Cox, Arlo Lewis, Jim Renshaw, Erv Malnirich, Jack Becker, Jack Nygaard, Dewey Moore, Ferg Nelson, Wayne England, Stan Tappen, Max Bitton, Eggs Beckley, John Booker, Parley Fox, Johnie Carrey, Tom Williams, Max Walker, Zeke West, Jack and Rollie Briggs,

Lon Jarvis, Dave Giles, Emerson Moody, Paul Kriley, Rex Lanham, Harry Vaughn, and Gordon Stimmell.

I thought sure I'd get the feeling that would be my poem for sure. But nothing yet has turned on the light so I'll let the old mind roam some more.

Next, I'll go to the horses I've known – there's got to be a poem in there. 'Cause most of these horses have packed me from here to everywhere.

There's Kenny, Henry, Lady, Sandy, Tony, Brownie, Shorty, Appy, Rowdy, Leppy, Suzy, Cindy, Dusty, Buddy, Betty, Brandy, Babe, Nig, Champ, Major, Deadeye, Popeye, Blaze, Goucho, Enoch, Marble, Star, Banjo, Runt, Queen, Fix, Joe, Torpedo, Bill, Icabod, Chief, Rex, Flicka, Checkers, Blue, Coon Dog, Badger, Tequilla, Jim Beam, Donna, Bess, Diltzy, and Midnight White.

The poem still won't get itself started with that idea I'm needing so bad. So now I'll go to the mules I've led down the trail – if that don't work I'll really be sad!

There's Johnie, Jerry, Jocko, Jack, Jingles, Josie, Jake, Margie, Molly, Maggie, Minnie, Mouse, Amos, Beckey, By God, Ben, Bernadine, Charlie, Charlie, Doc, Festus, Frank, Gus, Kate, Lola, Pat, Mike, Rosie, Snowball, Tilley, Rita, Betsey, Hot Rod, and Sam.

Well the poem just won't come together so guess I'll just quit right now. My chance to be a famous I.O.G.A. poet just went down the drain (and HOW!).

Chapter 24

The Long Elk Hunt

This chapter is a collection of several different hunting trips covering eight or ten years all in the Central Idaho Mountains now known as the Frank Church Wilderness. The people on the trips changed a little on different years, but the nucleus of the group remained relatively constant.

My dad, Verl Potts and Gerald Twitchell, a neighboring rancher, hunted, farmed, and cowboyed for 20-plus years in the Lost River Valley. (This is a story on its own!) One year, dad went to a family reunion in Utah and guess who was there? – Gerald Twitchell – they found out they were distant cousins!

Anyway, back to the "group." We usually had a group of four or five. Gerald's son, Jerry, my wife, Joy, after we were married, plus on some years Boyd Theitten, the Lost River Game warden, Stan Johnson, Gerald's brother, Harold, Gus Stocks or Kenneth Kelly would round out the group.

Seldom did we have enough stock and would have been what we now call "Pilgrims." We were never sure where we were going or how to get there. Good news/bad news, "We're lost but we're making good time!"

I would be hard pressed to differentiate years/stock/people, etc., but the memorable stories and participants stick out like a sore thumb because I've told and retold these yarns a multitude of times through the years. (Just pretend this is one long hunt with different people coming and going.)

Because we were usually, no always, short of stock, we had to plan on sort of "living off the land." These guys had lived their lives that way, but to a first-trip, hungry all the time anyway, fourteen-year-old kid, it was a new experience.

On this trip we had hauled the horses to the end of the road below Shoup, a place that is now called Corn Creek. The road then, about 1948, ended back upriver, a mile from where the boat ramp is now. The trail climbed up a hillside and through switchbacks down a steep shadowed hillside to the river.

After we had started down the shadowed side, we realized that the trail was frozen – glare ice would be more like it. At this point, we were committed with absolutely no way to stop and/or turn around. Now picture this – horses sliding behind you, trying for any footing to slow their momentum and about the second switchback seeing the river below with three or four horses floating in an eddy! Whoever had come through ahead of us had not had good luck to say the least. Nowadays, my term for that type of situation is "Puckerville City!"

Somehow, we made it down without losing any horses or people and headed down the river to Horse Creek where there was a pack bridge to the south side of the river. The bridge was one of the first ones built on the river and was pretty old. The sign on the bridge read: "Load Limit 10 Hd. (crossed out), 7 Hd. (crossed out), 3 Hd (not crossed out)." Out in the middle of the bridge, several of the two by eight boards had broken through from mules and horses' shoes cutting the wood away, not to mention you could look down through the holes fifty feet or so to the water.

I have no idea who, but someone in our group had hatched up a plan for our hunt. We would work our way up the trail on the south side of the river until we found a concentration of game and then we would camp and hunt. None of the participants had ever been there before; we had no map; we had only a vague idea of the country ahead. Keep in mind, we were going to "live off the land."

We were short of stock; we had seven head for five people. Two of the pack horses had a tent, stove, two food boxes and the sleeping bags. Back then, the small compact sleeping bags were thirty years from being developed. The bags were a combination of huge bedrolls and assorted blankets, pillows. And, we're going to hunt for a couple of weeks?

After two or three days of wandering along, we had used up the small amount of fresh meat in our larder. We had seen no sign of any edible mountain creatures. Things were definitely not working according to "The Plan."

My dad, a savvy woodsman and a good hunter, decided the reason we had seen no game was that we were too large a group; we were making too much noise, and we were not getting up early enough. Accordingly, he would head out on the trail before daylight, find some game to shoot, and have it ready to load on one of our riding horses when we came by later.

We got our group about ready to go when Gerald came up with a new idea. Nowadays, in my outfit, that is what is known as "Plan B." Because it was taking so long to roll up the sleeping bags and also making such a giant load on the mules, he decided to just drape all the bags over his saddle on his Pinto Stud Horse Pete. He would then find a tall rock or log to mount on top of the pile to hold them down and we would save all that time mantying and unmantying morning and night.

Now, the average thickness of each uncompressed bedroll was probably six or eight inches. When we finally got Gerald mounted, he was at least three feet above the level of the saddle and leading the two packhorses to boot. He reminded me of a camel jockey. Stud Horse Pete was gentle and taking to it with no problem.

We migrated along dad's route, listening for the anticipated rifle shot that would signal red meat to go with the rice and macaroni. I was the last rider in our little entourage with Gerald, the camel jockey, and the two mule packstrings directly ahead of me. I was looking around in all directions as my dad had taught me hoping to see a grouse or something to eat.

Lo and behold, about forty yards down the hill was a buck deer standing behind a tree with just his head sticking out. I looked around, but no one was looking my direction so that I could signal them. I was afraid if I whistled or said anything the deer would run off. I got off my horse, leaned up against a tree with my .30-30 and shot the deer in the head.

As soon as the gun went off, Gerald, riding along half asleep and Pete, walking along half asleep, became quite mobile! Pete jumped about four feet into the air, Gerald rolled off backward into the rocks from about ten feet up and was unleashing epitaphs even I had never heard before. Sleeping bags were raining out of the sky and fluttering to the ground.

The good thing about this was that I had gotten us some meat. If I had missed the deer, this story might never have been written. Eventually, it became a funny story in the years to come, but in that moment, things were more than a little tense. By the time we had the deer cleaned, the sleeping bags retrieved, etc., dad came trotting back down the trail to see what had happened. Gerald had sort of mellowed out by then and he laid it on thick to dad, "Yeah! 'Great White Hunter' goes out to get meat, walks by the only deer on the mountain, and his fourteen-year old kid has to shoot it."

By supper time, with liver and heart added to the meal and knowing that we had meat for the hunt, I had worked my way up to what I considered "Hero Status!"

We kept traveling along looking for this game concentration which seemed to be nonexistent. After several days, we ended up in the bottom of Papoose Creek, and although we had seen minimal game sign, we decided to hunt a few days at this spot. It was early afternoon and I was not the greatest help in setting up camp. So Dad said, "Stan, ride up the trail toward

Black Butte and see what you find for elk tracks."

I rode a mile or so up the hill where I saw a cow and calf track in the dust. I thought, "Boy, I'll tie up my Pinto mare, follow their tracks and shoot me an elk." I was following through on my plan and was taking my gun out of the scabbard when all hell broke loose. Trees were cracking and I heard the sound of a large animal coming toward us. I stepped back about six feet from my horse just as a giant bull elk came thundering at us. I lifted the gun and my mare was rearing up on the halter rope with the elk between us. I couldn't shoot and the elk turned down the hill still going full bore. I ran after him but was never able to get a shot. I came back to the mare about twenty minutes later and she was shaking so bad she could hardly stand up. I thought, "Wow, no wonder they say elk hunting is exciting!"

After a lifetime of hunting elk, I realize now that light-colored horses – whites, Pintos, grays, etc., are about the same color as an elk. That elk thought we were another bull and was in his charge and on us before he realized his mistake.

When I got back to camp that night, Kenneth Kelly and Gus Stocks had shot a big bull about a mile the other side of camp. The "Big Guys" went to retrieve the bull the next day, and I went back to look for the charger bull. I went a couple of miles past where he had charged us and the sun was just coming down the mountain. In the morning sunlight were two giant bulls or so I thought. I got off my horse, leaned against a tree and shot. After I tied up the mare, I went up to my "bull." I had a mule deer buck with nine points on one side and eight on the other! I couldn't afford to get him mounted, but hey, I would shoot a lot more and bigger in the coming years, right? No, he's still the best buck of my life!

We did finally find our way out of there with what was left of the "meat" buck, one six-point bull, and my nine by eight buck. Our last breakfast was meat and canned corn mixed with hotcake flour for hot cakes – no coffee, no syrup, no butter, no jam, and no sugar. We'd left a date cake in a sack of grain at the trail head; it didn't last long once we got to it.

We decided on one trip that we would try some new country. We started out on the same route as mentioned before, but went on down the river to Lance's Bar and camped up Little Squaw Creek. Now, these guys had managed to kill a few elk through the years and it had become somewhat of a ritual to do it according to camp policy. First, you only shot blue dry cows or spike bulls. Any shot was okay as long as it was no further than six inches behind the ears. In other words, you sneaked in close, made a good head or front neck shot so you wouldn't waste any meat. Failure to follow one or more of these rules would subject you to unrelenting camp ridicule.

My dad and I had paired up this day and we had gone up the ridge toward Eakin Cabin and then split up. He would go up the ridge another mile or two, drop down on the east side and hunt back toward me. I would drop down a quarter mile and hunt toward him. The weather was clear where we were, but river fog was slowly rising toward us. I had hunted along for an hour or so when I spied a big six-point bull across the canyon about 400 to 500 yards away. I still couldn't resist those horns! The fog had started rising pretty fast and was nearly to our level. I knew I had to shoot now or wait and hope the fog cleared later.

I was shooting a .30-06 Springfield and knew it would kill the elk from where I was. I got a solid rest and touched it off just as the fog engulfed the bull, with no way of knowing the result. I took off across the gully toward the direction of the bull. When I got there I found his tracks. He had walked forward from where I shot, turned around and backtracked across from where he stood when I shot. I had shot about six inches under his chest. It was still fogged in solid, maybe twenty to thirty foot visibility.

For lack of a better idea, I started following his tracks. About thirty or forty yards later, there he was, broadside looking at me. I pulled up on the side of his head and shot. He never even moved! I reloaded again, shot, saw some hair fly and he whirled and disappeared into the fog. I took off after him and paralleled him running full bore. I soon saw him running in the same direction about thirty yards away and shot him through the lungs.

Now, I'd committed two no-no's on one elk so I knew things wouldn't go smoothly when I got back to camp.

Twitchell had heard my shots and said, "What did you get – a nice dry cow?" I didn't answer. "A spike?" I still didn't answer. About then he grabbed the camp axe and took after me in a mock attack mode.

For the record, I went back to where my two empty bullets were and stepped it off to the patch of hair on the snow. Twelve steps! So far, I still hold the record of missing a bull at the closest distance of anyone I know.

We had some good luck in that area and returned with different groups of people for several years. One year Joy, my wife, was with us. We were hunting in late November and it was starting to get wintry. The snow was crusty and hard to sneak up on the elk. I told her we would go out in the early afternoon, find a place where the elk were feeding, and wait for the elk to feed toward our direction. We were on the east slope about 200 yards from a ridge top that the elk had used heavily the evening before.

A couple of hours before dark, we heard the elk walking, coming to feed in the crunchy snow. Six or eight cows fed above us, but we had to move a little to give Joy a rest for her gun. The snow was about two and one-half to three feet deep and Joy kept getting the gun barrel in the snow. I probably cleared it out with a stick three or four times before we got her a rest on the end of a log.

The plan was for her to shoot one and then I'd shoot another before they ran off. The mountain was very steep with tall bear grass under the snow. She shot a cow and I followed with another immediately. Both cows went down and started sliding toward us picking up speed every second and they were coming right at us. One was hurtling directly at us and I told Joy to run one way I'd run the other. The cow went between us within five feet of each of us and probably going thirty miles per hour! They continued down the mountain a couple hundred more yards, hit some trees and stopped.

We got them cleaned before dark and had a two-hour walk in the dark back to camp. We packed the hearts and livers back with us. The next morning we took some stock back to where we had left them and a large wolf had followed us licking the blood spots that had dripped in the snow as we walked back to camp the night before. Another one of those "phantom" wolves that did not exist until they hauled us in a bunch from Canada!

Another trip we went back into the Papoose Lake, Coyote Springs, Iodine Creek country in late November. For that high altitude we were way too late, but hey, we were pilgrims.

There was about two feet of frozen snow at Papoose Meadows and we were trying to scrape it off with a frying pan and skillets so we could set up our tent. Finally, we scraped the snow down to about one foot of solid ice. Consequently, we slowly melted our way down to the ground every time we built a fire. For some reason, Jerry Twitchell had forgotten his overshoes. (Back then shoes and overshoes were the accepted hunting footwear as snow pacs probably didn't even exist in someone's mind.) About the second day someone shot a doe deer for meat and her hide became part of the "plan." We had all seen pictures of the old mountain men with hide shoes/booties/leggings up around their knees. (See Introduction on page 9). The "plan" involved splitting the deer hide in two and lacing each half into overshoes for Jerry. As this was a new venture for all of us, it sounded logical to the hair side on the inside for warmth. (Still seems logical.)

We got him all strapped together and he made a test hike around camp. They worked great! Remember, we were camped in semi-level terrain. The next morning, Jerry and I worked our way around a long ridge and down into Iodine Creek where I killed a six-point bull. (I couldn't pass up those antlers again!) Jerry shot a cow through the shoulders with his .270, but she ran off. We had chunks of scapula bone from this exit hole three to four inches long, plus lung blood, so we were sure we would find her. Wrong! We followed her probably for two miles down Iodine Creek until she had totally quit bleeding. How? I still don't know. I've had others with lung blood that have gotten away. Evidently, if only one lung is hit and in the right circumstances, they are able to come out of it.

Anyway, we headed back toward camp and the weather had warmed up to melting temperatures. We had to go down a pretty steep hill for several hundred yards to camp and thereby created the problem. From the weight in the front going down hill, the deer hide overshoes stretched about two to three times Jerry's foot length and became very slick on the bottom. Somewhat, no, exactly like, skis. I will guarantee you that Jerry left some mighty wild tracks coming into camp, ricocheting off the trees, and tumbling down the mountain. I have become a pretty good tracker through the years, but I'll tell you if I had come upon his tracks and had known about the "Abominable Snow Man," I would have been sure I'd found one!

This has been a long elk hunt, but I thought some of it would make interesting reading.

*Interesting Footnote: This one hunt I went on was to be a short, easy elk hunt – five or six days at the most. Joy had stayed home with our two-month-old daughter, Kay. Twenty-eight days later I came home to find my suitcase and clothes all neatly piled by the front door. It was thereby decided (by mutual agreement) that Joy would go on all future elk hunts!

October 1, 1999, five days before the longest night.

Chapter 25

The Longest Night

On Wednesday, Oct. 7, 1999, Holton Quinn and I were hunting elk in Upper Stoddard Creek when I had the misfortune of taking a very hard fall into a patch of rocks hidden by chaparral and burnt limbs and trees. The fall happened around 12:30 p.m., and I hit the rocks with such force that I was unable to talk or breathe for quite awhile. All I could do was scream with pain in my right chest and lungs.

After about one hour with Holt helping me, I was able to prop myself up on a walking stick and my legs. I could feel my lung starting to fill with fluid, and I knew I was in bad trouble.

There was nowhere close that Holton could direct a helicopter rescue crew to land and, more importantly, nowhere that we could build a fire to keep me warm and reduce the inevitable shock. We decided to try and get me to a place where we could build a fire that would last for many hours and that the rescue crew would be able to chain saw dead trees down to land near where I was. We had about six or seven hours of daylight to get me there, and the distance was about two miles – normally about a one hour walk.

With Holton packing both rifles, all our stuff and my belt saw, he blazed trail, coming back to help me over logs, under logs and around logs.

Just at dark we made it to where we had left the horses that morning.

Holton helped me get as comfortable as possible. He lit a pitch stump afire, filled our water jugs and left his extra coats before heading to our camp for sleeping bags, foam pads, food, more medicine, etc.

During the time Holt was gone, I had to lay close enough to the fire for warmth – probably about eight feet – but the stump was burning in such a manner that there was six or eight upright slabs that would burn off eventually and fall outward. If I was in the wrong place they could fall on me, so it was a guessing game to try to guess which side to be on. Not easy, when I could only push myself backward with my hands and chin. The pain and stiffness being so bad that I could not get up to my knees.

Time seemed to stand completely still. I would slowly count to 100 and back, thinking that would get me several minutes closer to morning. I would look at my watch and very seldom would over a minute have gone by.

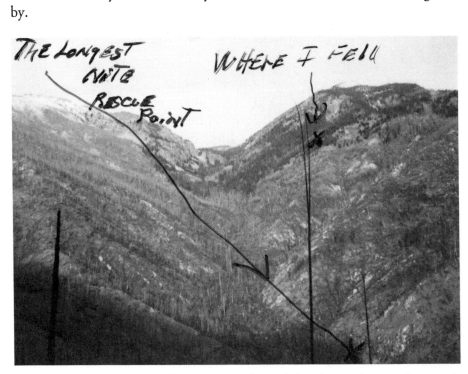

A diagram sketched against the mountain where I fell and was subsequently rescued.

Holt got back about 11 or 12 o'clock, and I was able to prop up against a log on the foam pad and cover up with my sleeping bag.

We decided that rather than Holt leaving for the river in the middle of the night to wait for daylight to see if there was any chance of me being able to get on the horse. As daylight finally approached, I realized that could not happen, and Holt left with both horses as soon as he could see.

I told him it was about five and one-half hours to the river. He made it in five, and he and Joy were able to get the Forest Service helicopter from Indianola.

I heard it coming at about 2:30 p.m. on Thursday afternoon – about twenty-six hours after my fall, and definitely my longest night.

The helicopter took me to Salmon where the emergency room doctor, Dr. Meyers, put a drain tube in my lung and called another life-flight to take me to the Idaho Falls Regional Medical Center where they had better and more extensive facilities to treat and care for me as I was in pretty bad shape.

The x-rays there found that I had broken eleven ribs, plus the punctured lung and BLOOD IN THE HEART SAC! They did what I think was called a femural aerotagram and after some very anxious minutes

Where I spent the "longest night" and they cleared the trees so the rescue helicopter could land and pick me up.

found it was not leaking. If it had been leaking, the options were not good.

1. Operate with one chance in three of survival, or,
2. Don't operate and die.

They had the surgical team all ready when they finally found out for sure it was not leaking and Joy and I, plus our three daughters, heaved a collective sigh of relief.

It was six days in intensive care – home to recuperate for three months – then a shoulder surgery repair and another three months of therapy and exercise.

I packed, guided and cooked at the hunting camps last fall and feel very lucky to be able to get back in the country that I love. On October 6, 2000, I took a "walk-about" to celebrate my survival – overmatched myself, as usual, but felt great to be able to do it.

The helicopter rescue crew carved this while waiting for the chopper to return for them.

Stan Potts with grandson Tim Maxfield, each with a separated shoulder – grandson Tim and a snowboard, the Old Guy and rocks!

Verl Potts and his little brother Merle's grave about seventy-five years after the baby's death. Dad said the tree was about two inches in diameter when they buried Merle.

Stan Potts and Jerry Black with the plaque we had made for Dad's baby brother. Jenny and Jay Black in the foreground.

Five generations of the Potts family. Clockwise from front center: 94-year-old Ethel Coburn; Kay Potts Black, great-granddaughter; Joy Potts, my wife; Robyn Potts Maxfield, great-granddaughter; Jerry Maxfield; Sarah Potts, my mother; Stanley Potts, holding Jeny Black, great-great-granddaughter; Jay Black, great-great-grandson, held by Stani Potts, great-granddaughter; and Verl Potts, (Ethel Coburn's son and my father).

FOR ADDITIONAL COPIES

Additional copies of **The Potts' Factor Versus Murphy's Law** *are available from the author in either softcover or hardcover format at the address listed below. Please enclose $23.50 for a postpaid softcover copy or $28.50 for a postpaid hardcover copy.*

STANLEY POTTS
4 Redside Way
Shoup, Idaho 83469